To KNOW the PLACE

To Ellen

Gary A Wright

To KNOW the PLACE

An Anthropologist Remembers A Michigan Town

Gary A. Wright

ANDREWS UNIVERSITY PRESS
BERRIEN SPRINGS, MICHIGAN
1999

This book is dedicated to my great grandmother, Mary Hoopingarner, and to my mother Margaret Miller (nee Hoopingarner) who alone can attest to its accuracy.

© August 20,1999 ANDREWS UNIVERSITY PRESS
213 Information Services Building
Berrien Springs, MI 49104-1700
616-471-6915
aupress@andrews.edu
http://www.andrews.edu/AUPress

Library of Congress Cataloging-in-Publication Data
Wright, Gary A.
        To know the place: an anthropologist remembers a Michigan town /
Gary A. Wright.
                p.   cm.
        Includes bibliographical references and index.
        ISBN 1-883925-23-1 (pbk.)
        1. Berrien Springs (Mich.)--Social life and customs. 2. Middle West--
Social life and customs. 3. United States--Social life and customs--1945-
1970. 4. Wright, Gary, A.--Childhood and youth. 5. Anthropologists--United
States Biography. I. Title.
F574.B47W75   1999
977.4'11--dc21

Acknowledgements

A work such as this is never accomplished in isolation. My university colleagues and our students provided consistent intellectual stimulation, allowing me to try out ideas and points of view. They could be critical, but were always supportive. Our interlibrary loan service obtained far more books and articles than are listed in the bibliography, and I thank them for their efforts and attention; they were completely indispensable.

I appreciate the comments of all of the reviewers, even when I disagreed with them because they forced me to clarify. Robert Myers of the Berrien County Historical Association provided information and pleasant conversation. I wish to thank Bob for catching errors in historical fact and supplying many of the photographs. I am also grateful to Dr. Øystein LaBianca of Andrews University for championing the manuscript and for his excavations at Tell Hesban.

Carol Loree, Director of the Andrews University Press, had faith that the manuscript could be worked into shape. Her associate, Deborah Everhart, faced the daunting task of convincing me that jumbles of words could be formed into readable sentences.

Finally, I thank my high-school teachers and classmates for providing the experiences.

We shall not cease from exploration
And the end of all our exploring
Will be to arrive where we started
And know the place for the first time.
Through the unknown, remembered gate
When the last of earth left to discover
Is that which was the beginning;
At the source of the longest river
The voice of the hidden waterfall
And the children in the apple-tree
Not known, because not looked for
But heard, half-heard, in the stillness
Between two waves of the sea.
Quick now, here, now, always —
A condition of complete simplicity
(Costing not less than everything)
And all shall be well and
All manner of thing shall be well
When the tongues of flame are in-folded
Into the crowned knot of fire
And the fire and the rose are one.

Book and chapter titles are taken from *Four Quartets* by T. S. Eliot.

Home Is Where One Starts From

*D*uring the heat of one August afternoon, following the complaints of my daughter that her room was too hot, I installed an old Whirlpool air conditioner in her window. It didn't work. I called their 800 number in St. Joseph, Michigan, for repairs, asked for advice, and was put on hold. For nearly half an hour I waited for the air-conditioner specialist to come on the line. But it was not a sojourn to Michigan in silence. I was treated to canned home-improvement messages: ways to keep my home warm in winter and cool in summer; tips on sewing clothes; and instructions for preparing nutritious, but still good tasting, recipes. Eventually, I began to notice the peculiar lilt to the speech patterns—almost a song presented in solo female voices. It was my native dialect.

For those who travel extensively, as I have been fortunate to do since I left high school and my hometown in 1958, the way people speak is one cultural trait that impresses itself upon us immediately. What we recognize need not be a completely foreign tongue, such as Turkish; it may be as minimal as the local generic term for a soft drink: pop in the Midwest, soda in the East, and coke on the coast of Mississippi. Everywhere we journey, we must learn to converse with strangers by employing new words, substituting different meanings, and rearranging rhythms and cadences of our familiar speech patterns to assimilate yet another dialect of a language in which we thought we were already fluent.

Growing up during the early to mid-1950s in the small, farm town of Berrien Springs, Michigan, I acquired particular habits of speaking that seemed normal and natural to me. A bonnet was an item of clothing that a woman wore on her head as protection from the sun. A soda included a scoop of ice cream, normally vanilla. It was a surprise to learn that a boot could also be the trunk of a car and that "y'all" could refer to only one individual under direct address. Small difficulties to overcome, perhaps. But how could I, at the age of 16 in that geographical context, have understood that the construction "the horse kicked the man in the head" was impossible to phrase directly in Navaho? That was something I was to learn years later.

On the surface, Midwesterners, such as I, seem to speak a mutually intelligible dialect of the English language, eat many of the same foods prepared in similar if not identical ways, and interact with our parents, children, and other kin in a manner not unlike that of my eastern students. Though Midwesterners may not be fully the cultural other to these upstate New York youths, our small degree of foreignness provides a sufficient number of examples of diversity at the introductory level. I knew more about the people and the cultural forms of the United States' heartland than I did about Southerners from Dixie, native Californians, or New Englanders—enough at least to find plentiful instances of these types of cultural variability nestled comfortably, if still deeply, in our own midst.

American culture, as a system, obviously differs from all others throughout the world. It exhibits great internal variability even today despite the homogenizing effects of cable television and the ease of travel from one coast or region of the United States to any other. We do not all behave in identical fashions. Midwesterners, for example, do not robustly hug and kiss across the genders as a usual part of the ritual greeting, and most certainly not upon being introduced for the first time. Yet, this ritual greeting is common (and even after more than 20 years of residence in New York State still bothersome to me) among many Easterners. Neither do we Midwesterners blithely inquire about people's salaries—or what they paid for their houses or their new cars—immediately upon meeting them at a social gathering. Yet these, too, seem to be common everyday behavioral traits that our fellow upstate New Yorkers appear to find completely normal, and wholly acceptable, cultural practices.

A host of significant historical reasons exists for this cultural variability. The Middle West was settled at a later time in our nation's past, as compared to the East Coast, and often by different ethnic groups who faced dissimilar social and economic problems upon arrival in their new homeland. For me to come to grips with this diversity, it seemed logical to place cultural events into their specific historical contexts. Since I had grown up in Berrien Springs during the 1950s and had left Ann Arbor and the University of Michigan (where I first arrived in 1958) by the late 1960s, migrating slowly eastward, this temporal period appeared to be the most logical one from which to draw my examples.

The year 1956 was extremely special to my hometown because it celebrated the 125th anniversary of its founding. The celebration involved four days of parades and speeches. A special edition (June 20, 1956) of the village weekly newspaper (*The Journal Era*) was printed, and multi-page spreads appeared in dailies from local urban centers—far-away, exotic locales such as South Bend, Indiana, some 20 miles to the south. This date, thus, served as a more focused point from which to launch my inquiry.

As I began to construct my classroom public narratives, however, I came to realize with some small degree of panic that specific details of United States and world history did not easily surface—even those of events that occurred while I was growing up in the mid-1950s. On the one hand, I could vividly recall experiencing the dramatic impact of the rising phenomenon named Elvis Presley when he made his first national appearance on television on Tommy and Jimmy Dorsey's "Stage Show" in January of 1956. (Presley would sell 13.5 million singles and 3.75 million albums in 1956 alone.) Yet, the majority of world happenings remained far too shadowy in my memory. Did none of them affect me in any way while I was in high school, not even to the point that I could bring them readily to the forefront?

We certainly must have been aware of the Soviet Union's invasion of Hungary, Khruschchev's angry denunciation of Stalin for his depredations upon the peoples of the Soviet Union, and the British/French/Israeli attack on Egypt over control of the Suez Canal. Each of these major international news stories occurred in 1956. Yet as I read about these events nearly 40 years later, nothing crashes back into my mind—no context and no memory of where I was or what I was doing when the news descended upon my teenage ears.

I have the uneasy impression that I must have grown up so entirely isolated that the world beyond the United States could not and did not much intrude. I am sure that this is not completely accurate. Still, it does manage to convey a sense of small-town,

1950s America. Despite earth-shattering global events and the constant specter of menacing Communism presented to us incessantly through the media and the A-Bomb drills that we frequently practiced in our school ("under your desks with your heads between your knees, please, and quickly now"), the international scene does not appear to have occupied inordinate amounts of our waking hours.

I think that we were slightly more aware of the national scene because it impinged more immediately upon our daily lives. The bus boycott in Montgomery, Alabama, began in 1955 when Rosa Parks refused to give up her seat to a white patron, and it lasted until the end of December in 1956. That event was attended by a vivid outpouring of racial hatred and included the massive white resistance to the attempts undertaken by African-Americans to integrate the southern segregated schools (all filmed in black and white for the television news programs). It became a topic that we did recognize and discuss. Berrien County did have integrated schools; the nearby town of Benton Harbor was the prime example. In 1955, Thurgood Marshall of the NAACP attacked the Benton Harbor School Board over its proposal to build new schools which, he argued, would create two separate but equal (one black and one white) school systems. Yet, at that time, only about 10 percent of the high-school graduating class in Benton Harbor was African-American.

We had the normal (and shameful) prejudices for that era, but we precipitated no ugly public, racial incidents—no Little Rocks—that would bring the national press corps to our seemingly well-hidden, tucked-away corner of the world.

Before the early 1950s, our own town and a few surrounding communities constituted our operative world. But by the mid-1950s, television began to create a larger, and new, environment with a host of sights and sounds while we reclined on the sofa. Our smugness began to evaporate in black-and-white pictures. Live action was not always possible—"film at 11:00" was more the norm. And our town, being bombarded with this new medium, no longer seemed quite so physically isolated from the world outside. That spatial shield would be further diminished with the enactment of the Interstate Highway System Bill, properly the "Highway Act of 1956." I had seen neither the Pennsylvania Turnpike nor the New York State Thruway. It took nearly five hours to drive on two-lane roads to Ann Arbor, about 150 miles to the east. That trip by the mid-60s could be completed in half that time.

Dwight David Eisenhower was our nation's president. If the American nation, Berrien County included, could again over-whelmingly "Like Ike" in that year's national election rather than Adlai Stevenson (my mother was a rabid Democrat), it was, in part, because we could not in our wildest fantasies imagine him sleeping with Kim Novak or Marilyn Monroe or seeking political advice from Frank Sinatra or Roy Rogers (or even from that minor actor Ronald Reagan for that matter). If Ike had his sever-al indiscretions, too, they were performed in great secret and, if discovered by the press, remained completely suppressed by the mute Fourth Estate. His public actions could not have conceiv-ably paved the way to a sexual revolution, something that would have made him far more politically attractive and, ultimately, worth admiring by a 16-year-old male adolescent in 1956. In short, President Eisenhower was a wholly comfortable figure as the country's leader, equally at home on his favorite golf links as he was as general on the battlefields of Europe. The nation's course would be steady: onward but always, in a teenager's eyes, smooth and even.

This revolutionary role as cultural hero was to be left to John F. Kennedy early in the following decade, a man of whom I was totally unaware in 1956. Unlike Kennedy, Ike was not the direct descendent of King Arthur in our minds. And nowhere in the United States, at least that any of my peers or I knew of first hand, was there a true Camelot. Ike was a solid, dependable, and unex-citing chieftain. He was a symbol of cultural stability, a man who was neither a throwback nor a visionary.

Notwithstanding the looming specter of Communism and the daily threat of all-out atomic annihilation, we did believe in a future. We vaguely anticipated it even while we actively resisted what I presume today to have been an almost minimal effort of our teachers and parents to prepare us for time to come. Our lack of overt interest, I believe now, stemmed largely from the excite-ment of the present. We were "teenagers" (there were some thir-teen million of us nationwide), a status term that had just come into popularity in the late 1940s. We would begin to develop our own separate subculture—hip language, extravagant hairstyles (ducktails), wild music (rock and roll), and new and outrageous, but extremely cool, behaviors. We would be the first daring and wholly independent generation in American history. What we did not realize, of course, was that this same cultural revolution had been attempted unsuccessfully by countless numbers of young people in this country on many occasions long before us.

Rock and roll was just bursting onto the American scene, and television—still in its infancy—brought Elvis and Dick Clark (1957) directly into our living rooms. We all had our driver's licenses by the age of 16. We drove the farm pick-up trucks or the newly manufactured V-8 Chevrolets customized with dual exhausts, dual antennas, chopped and channeled bodies, sporty fender skirts, and all the extras that could be built on. We were a new generation, breaking totally free from the confining bondage of the past (about which we knew precious little anyway).

The past of my county and my hometown was never communicated to us beyond what old stories the adults might relate to us as an aside—a chance comment simply in passing during an odd moment of repose. But this retelling was never undertaken in any formal sessions of instruction in any high-school classroom or even more informally through the medium of tales concerning the heroic acts and deeds of our forebears. Our pioneer ancestors had apparently been (conveniently?) forgotten as individual heroes within just slightly more than a century. It was as if history, particularly the local variety, no longer mattered. My hometown's past, if not dead and buried with formal honors in a stirring public ritual, was at least certainly deemed irrelevant.

"History is bunk," Henry Ford (from Michigan) is alleged to have once remarked. Whether the town's elders felt the same way or not, I cannot say. I can only assume that, since these residents were so completely secure in their own basic cultural traditions, long-ago events never needed to be articulated in a more stilted, academic-like fashion.

Thus, as I look back, I feel as if I grew up in a setting that only scarcely acknowledged the linear concept of time. We had no local historical society of which I was aware. A specific time-oriented, worthwhile, and relatable past did not seem to exist for my own hometown—at least one was never clearly articulated to us.

The only event that I can clearly remember being commemorated by the entire village was Memorial Day (or Decoration Day as we referred to it). This annual, ritual occasion required a totally different concept of time—one that is cyclical. Its renewal each year was always accompanied by a parade led by the high-school marching band dutifully followed by the local Boy Scout and Girl Scout troops, the Woodmen of the World with their fake axes snugly nestled upon their shoulders, the American Legion and the Women's Auxiliary, and our two fire trucks and sole police car. Inevitably, there was also extensive, heart-lifting, patriotic oratory. Its ending was signaled by the discharging of rifles at Rose Hill Cemetery on the edge of town by the uniformed and bemedaled American Legion survivors of foreign wars. To this day, I am still emotionally moved by the music of marching bands in any parade. So that, at least, did have one lasting, and wholly positive, effect on me.

This, then, is a personal history of one place because it is within this specific matrix that my own eventual maturation took place. What was important to me then and how I learned to behave properly, as a white male and a small-town Midwesterner, were based upon more than a century of cultural traditions. They were successful for the townspeople, the white males at least, of a small Midwestern country village at mid-century because these behaviors were well-worn through experience. They were visible daily actions that could be transmitted to us orally while we actually participated in them. We learned by emulating and by listening. And while we rebelled, it was merely a rebellion of music, cars, and language—never an outright rejection of the moral values which we stretched but never intended to reject. These precepts were set in me for life, and I still appreciate and defend them some forty years later.

I have tried, usually in vain, to balance both rebellion and values in my own research and academic career which is now well beyond its 30th anniversary. During these three decades, I have been actively engaged in creating pasts for other peoples in other places, other times, other cultures. My field research in prehistoric archeology has taken me to four of the world's continents, and I have extensively studied and analyzed the archeological records and ethnohistoric documents of both Native Americans and ancient Middle Easterners. These research findings have been transmitted not only to my peers in published form but also orally to several generations of my students, both graduates and undergraduates, in lectures, seminars, and shouting matches in bars from Jackson, Wyoming, to Bordeaux, France.

No such research undertaking is ever successfully accomplished in an intellectual vacuum. Science is not, and certainly never can be, a value-free system of inquiry. Our personal and cultural pasts, including mine most assuredly, impinge directly upon our interpretations of events that have already transpired. We view the bits and pieces of evidence through multicolored, distorted lenses. Any single event from the past may denote many different meanings, each depending upon the cultural context of the specific viewer. And a major portion of this context depends upon the place within which it was constructed.

This search for the past of the cultural other is a particularly Euro-American obsession. Ethnic peoples elsewhere are normally content with their own unique histories, and they exhibit little abiding interest in anyone else's past. Clearly, then, in my ongoing quest, I am a true product of my own specific cultural world and not the ones that I am seeking to reconstruct. Thus, in order for me to assess my work in retrospect, I must first reflect upon my own past. I must interpret my own ghosts and place them into an understandable cosmic order. My narrative can be neither strictly linear nor ethnographic in voice. It must shift to whichever seems germane because the past, both our own and that of our place, is never far from the present. Both call simultaneously, and they must be recognized and answered. Returning and regenerating, time ago informs, guides, and haunts us.

In the Edgware Road

You gain the first distinct impression of gently merging into the Middle West, at least geographically if not yet culturally, once you pass Cleveland heading westward. Crossing the Lake Erie basin, the land is flat and the cornfields stretch endlessly all the way to Iowa where they are then almost imperceptively replaced by wheat and open range in Nebraska. The skyline from Cleveland onward to the front range of the Rocky Mountains, which along I-80 begins at Cheyenne, Wyoming, is broken only by lonesome grain elevators, occasional small towns, and even fewer urban enclaves such as Chicago and Omaha. However, instead of continuing directly on toward the setting sun, drive northward from Toledo, say some 50 miles, deep into southern Michigan. Here I-94 slashes east-west across the southern portion of the state, providing another kind of vista: heavily cut-over, second-growth deciduous forests; dense, brushy, and tangled understory; small 80-acre family farms; and constantly interrupted views.

Berrien County, in extreme southwestern Michigan, lies uncomfortably wedged between Lake Michigan to the west, the northern boundary of Indiana to the south, and the rest of Michigan. Territory-wise, as part of Michigan, it should be properly classified as belonging to the industrialized east. Yet, it has been farm country from the time of the first intensive settlement by white Americans in the 1830s, and its own urban self-identification has been with Chicago—the hog butcher to the world—and not with Detroit, the automobile capital. Thus, as boys, we lived (and we suffered) with the Cubs and Bears rather than with the Lions and Tigers. If there were too many trees and hills and not enough tornados to be called Kansas, it was still solidly

9

Midwestern in its cultural orientation and its traditional beliefs concerning its own unique past.

Growing up in the 50s, I was never ill-at-ease with Berrien County's past—probably because I knew so little about it. We had courses in world history, American history, and Michigan history, but I cannot say that any of us ever learned very much about these subjects despite what I still prefer to think were the honest efforts of most of our high-school teachers. We had to recite the presidents in order—I could successfully make it to Jefferson. Our instructors would unceasingly remind us that the information about the past that we were being called upon to memorize was relevant to our future lives, and, hence, was of great importance to us. However, they could never satisfactorily convince us precisely why this might be true, and neither did they ever make anything beyond the most minimal attempt to do so.

I came away with very little basic knowledge from those high-school history classes. Nothing was ever debated or really discussed; it was just pure rote—names, dates, dynasties, presidents, wars, and rumors of wars. It was never impressed upon us that history is worth thinking about—that the past is worth thinking with. For example, Berrien Springs was initially called Wolf Prairie: But why? Why was the name changed? Who was Berrien anyway? A person or a thing? And where were (are) these elusive springs? Was there some ulterior motive behind the failure of our teachers to consider the town's, or even the county's, past? Even worse, was there some reason why we were not to know these matters? Were these dangerous facts, ones that would lead us down the wrong future path? Or was it simply knowledge of no discernible social or aesthetic value?

I am not suggesting that any school boy should leap from bed on a warm summer morning and say to himself, "Today, I am going to worry about why Berrien Springs is no longer called Wolf Prairie." Certainly, in my opinion, he would be far better off spending the day trying to learn how to hit a curve ball. And yet, the questions remain: Why was the name changed? Why does Berrien County identify culturally with the Middle West? Even more importantly, why should the past concern us at all?

Simply put, the past establishes our traditions and simultaneously provides a justification for them. We are not merely comfortable with our own traditional ways of doing things—we are comfortable with our cultural past itself. Yet, we can change our past because we actively create it. I am not writing here about changing the actual events—Berrien Springs was once Wolf Prairie. What I am concerned with is our interpretation of the meaning of those events. What is the context of those events both then and, more importantly, now? That's thinking with the past. Specific events of the past are thought about in the context of the present and become the hardcore data set we use to create both the world around us and the traditions that we live for and by. Hence, the past both informs us and reforms us.

It is this past as heritage that makes Berrien Springs rural and pastoral (Middle Western) rather than urban and industrial (Eastern). The earliest white American settlers, from whom many of today's Midwesterners directly descend—culturally if not always biologically—migrated into the region from the late 1820s and 1830s until well after mid-century. These ancestors were farmers, most of them German, English, or Irish in background. They streamed into the old Northwest Territory, a geographic entity which would later form the core of what we now call the Middle West. It was at that time a land possessing little or no written history and certainly no cultural past that would have either impressed or interested these white pioneers.

The settlers not only displaced the original Native American inhabitants, whose own heritage was wild (rather than rural); at the same time, these homesteaders also effectively erased the Native Americans' unique past from active white memory. In the process, these Euro-Americans created a new set of traditions for themselves. This past they considered to be historical (factual) rather than mythical (fantasy). Myths and tales were the typical methods by which Native Americans readily recalled their own significant events to memory. The newly arriving immigrants—primarily from Central Europe—were escaping not only a less-than-successful present but also segments of their past that they no longer found useful or even pleasant enough to preserve through time with ritual retelling.

These carefully selected memories of the first American settlers enable future generations to recreate again—oftentimes as an historic, but lost, golden age. This is not unlike the Achaean warrior society of Homer's *Iliad*—one to strive for but one forever unattainable. This newly invented past would become the justification for the historical traditions of ruralism, self-reliance, and rugged individualism. These, according to this basic underlying myth of American history, were originally engendered on the nineteenth-century, Midwestern frontier. No people's concept of their own history can be expressed simply as a straight temporal line. It is a never-ending circle, one that returns periodically upon itself for renewal and revitalization.

The Midwest projects this consistent image even today. When I ask my undergraduates how they perceive this region of the United States, both its people and its way of life, I receive the following most typical descriptions: rural, agrarian, friendly, traditional, individual, honest, conservative, and naive. Particularly naive! If a similar poll had been taken in 1956 among typical college students in any upstate New York academic setting, I have no doubt that the very same impressions would have been recorded.

Yet, how could it be otherwise? After all, most non-Midwesterners' first introduction to this region as little children was through the movie *The Wizard of Oz*. All of the action that takes place directly in Kansas—the very heartland of the Middle West—is filmed in black and white. (In 1900, the author, L. Frank Baum, introduced Kansas on the first page of his book as that "great gray prairie.") This cinematic technique presents the viewer with a stark contrast: the natural (full-color), wonderful, and exciting environment of the Land of Oz, but also most peoples'—particularly those of the youngsters who are captivated by the film—normal world. Like Kansas and its farm life, Dorothy's Aunt Em, Uncle Henry, and the hired hands are depicted as thoroughly honest people, but people who are definitely dull and drab—a virtually lifeless gray. Again, when Dorothy and her dog Toto are embroiled in the controversy with her teacher that opens the movie, the adults all uniformly side with law and order rather than with the small child despite their clear sympathy for her agonizing plight. Finally, the weather in Kansas is simply awful. It culminates in a violent tornado that spirits Dorothy away from her safe homeland to an entirely alien culture.

Further, it is the wicked witch of the East who is killed by the falling house, and her sister (Dorothy's sworn enemy) is from west of the Land of Oz. Hence, East and West are both symbolized as dangerous directions for Dorothy. In real life, to a Jayhawker, the former is urban and industrialized while the latter is still wild and unsettled (rather than rural and pastoral like Kansas). Glinda is a good witch and lives in the North which must be a nice place; yet Glinda's sister from the South, although probably also a good witch, is never formally introduced to us. Indeed, we never encounter her person at all (ambivalence?). And despite young Dorothy's initial fascination with the Emerald City's culture and values, her primary goal is always to escape from its current of intrigue and return to the quiet prairies of her Middle Western homeland.

Thus, Oz, like Kansas situated in the heartland of the Middle West, is in the center of the universe and is completely surrounded by both good and evil. Kansas is conservative but safe to a small farm girl. On the other hand, one of the film's primary messages is obvious: the Midwest is clearly not a place to be, or, by extension, to be from.

In essence, then, Middle Westerners as a people are typified as the yeoman farming class of the United States, and my students' perceptions are accurate as far as they go. When the Continental Congress' Land Ordinance of 1785 mandated that the Northwest Territory be surveyed in regular and seemingly monotonous six-mile squares, the result was straight boundaries, straight roads, and even straighter people. "Naive" will do nicely!

Thus, knowing nothing about these weighty historical matters, I could grow up being comfortable with Berrien County's past. Certainly, as I noted, my ease was not based upon knowledge that my high-school teachers were likely to force upon us. The Midwest, and hence Berrien County and probably the rest of the United States for that matter, generally believed that it drew its most cherished moral and cultural values from the frontier experiences of those nineteenth-century men and women (both white and American) who pioneered west of the Allegheny Mountains. This was a heritage with which any school boy could be at ease, even if the concept was never made explicit to us in a formal classroom. It was history as implicit, cultural knowledge.

The closest that I ever came to these pioneer days was one Saturday night when my mother was out of town. We lived with my great grandmother, Mary Hoopingarner (1866-1962). I used this occasion to host a small beer party for my friends. About a dozen of us, all sixteen to seventeen years of age, made up the group. I like to think that my grandmother, being nearly blind and deaf, was unaware of the drinking. We sat around her rocking chair in a circle on the floor. She related stories of her youth, some 80 years earlier, including a vivid account of coming to Michigan in a covered wagon. Her tales of homesteading—of 16- to 18-hour days clearing farmland, planting, cooking for the hands, butchering, canning, and sewing—with its hardships and joys held us spellbound for hours. Some 40 years later, that evening still leaves a deep impression upon me. Fundamental values of hard work and individualism were imparted to us through her stories. As the designated "keeper of the nation's values," the Midwest now seems hopelessly out of date. The shepherd, heavily overburdened with his pastoral outlook, is a dull companion unless you, too, are a country hick.

As I began, some years ago, to read Berrien County histories, I was struck by how the telling of that past and the actual literary techniques employed by the writers had changed. At the turn of the century, when there were fewer than 100 years of a story to recount, authors would spend the initial 35 to 40 percent of their monograph on a brief narrative beginning with the first French (white) explorers followed by the British and then the American settlers. The remainder of the weighty volume would consist of biographies of the county's leading residents, past and present. (In some such county histories, individuals even paid the author a fee to be included; I don't know if that was the case in Berrien County.) The volume *Portrait and Biographical Record of Berrien and Cass Counties* (1893) is dedicated solely to the personal biographies of more than 400 of its apparently most typical and worthy citizens and pioneers. Such early books and their particular genre stand as a monument to the creation of instant history, a symbolic achievement so necessary in this region during the late nineteenth century. These tales of the past must be true because they were recorded, as it were, on stone as the written (and received) word.

This literary method served to accomplish two things. First, by focusing initially on the French explorers, the writers successfully removed American Indians from any meaningful role in the present and in all of the future presents to come. References might be made to Native Americans in passing; but in general, as an ethnic group, they were almost completely ignored. There were a few notable exceptions. In Berrien County, for example, were the two Pokagons, father and son, who were Potawatomi. These two Native American males could be safely placed in a cultural context well after the onset of Euro-American immigration into the area. Simon, the son, was educated at Notre Dame University. He was a published author and a frequently sought-after orator; hence, in the eyes of the late nineteenth-century white public, he had become partially civilized. (Yet, who, for instance, was Mocassin, the Potawatomi after whom Mocassin Bluff near

Buchanan is named?) Being denied their own history, the Native Americans were totally disenfranchised from all future generations on the land. By the 1870s they were invisible people and virtually have remained as such. Even as late as 1956 when I found myself playing basketball against one Native American whose family had managed to persevere and survive intact into the mid-twentieth century, I had no curiosity.

Secondly, by focusing on the living or recently deceased white immigrants, the historical narratives firmly established traditional bona fides. Future white generations had both a stake and a historically secure place in the land. It was theirs not only by right of conquest over a nameless and by now already forgotten foe. It was also theirs by right of direct descent from their pioneer kinfolk, many of whom (or their children) still lived right next door. History was neighborly and still alive orally. The biographies of these carefully selected worthies (by their higher social status and ready cash) provided a direct generational and kinship link as well as a lifestyle (a tradition) to which those who came after them must constantly aspire.

Even today, a full century later, these narratives may serve to bind our own personal lives directly with the past. In 1886, my maternal great grandfather, John C. Hoopingarner (1858-1929), came to Berrien Springs from Butler, Indiana. Coolidge writes of him in 1906: "In 1888, Mr. Hoopenganer [sic] was married to Miss Mary Hastings [my pioneer great grandmother who helped raise me], a daughter of James Hasting [sic—a maternal great, great grandfather whom I never knew], and unto them have been born two sons, John [my maternal grandfather and town postmaster] and Charles [a great uncle and a mail carrier in South Bend]. By a former marriage Mr. Hoopenganer [sic] had two daughters: Maud [a great aunt], now the wife of Dr. Warren A. Smith [my family doctor as a small child, whom she had already divorced]; and Millie [actually Nellie, my great aunt], who is assistant postmistress at Berrien Springs [who in 1956 was retired and lived in Napannee, Indiana]." My aunts and uncles were the offspring of this pioneer family, making the next generation my cousins. Some of them lived nearby and interacted with me on an almost daily basis. Thus, in this single terse paragraph, I discovered an instant past that was uniquely my own. Despite errors, Coolidge through the written word had helped to link me with my own forebears.

When the elder John migrated north to Berrien Springs, he went into business managing a local hotel. He later traded this hostelry for the house that I grew up in, a massive stone-block structure with 13 rooms including six bedrooms, a dining room that could accommodate more than a dozen simultaneous feasters, and a walk-in pantry. A quarter of a century after his death, his wife, my great grandmother Mary, continued to operate a boarding house. By the early 1950s one boarder remained, a middle-aged spinster named June (who eventually did marry) who was the secretary at Hilltop Coal and Ice, the company that supplied the coal for our furnace.

The local histories of today are often far less personal, totally lacking in this narrative intimacy and being more argumentative in their style; and biographies, such as a recent one on Benjamin Purnell (*Brother Benjamin: A History of the Israelite House of David* by Clare E. Adkin), are reserved for full-length treatments. While names and dates appear—John Pike as Berrien Springs' initial homesteader in the summer of 1829—the narratives are event-oriented. We read of the "Bridgman Red" trial of 1923, the building of the courthouse in Berrien Springs, the history of Whirlpool Corporation, or the House of David baseball team. While these are interesting vignettes in themselves, the authors frequently fail

Benjamin Franklin Purnell (1861-1927)

to connect them to the lives or daily concerns of ordinary people or to their traditions. These events exist in space, on a white page of paper; but only by the efforts of our own mental gymnastics can we relate them to the linear time of our particular pasts.

When I read these histories, I sometimes feel very disassociated from the times being depicted. Present-day values are smeared across the historical canvas without any structure. Although these vague sketches create a recognizable picture for many of today's viewers, I suspect the scenes would have been largely unrecognizable to the participants themselves. The authors look back and at, rather than forward and from, the past. For example, when the Seventh Regiment of Michigan Militia under Colonel Alamanson Huston of Niles boarded the riverboat *Matilda Barney* in Berrien Springs during the Black Hawk War in 1832, Berrien County was in a state of near panic. Yet, if the actual fighting were being conducted several hundred miles away, why should this be the case? To answer this question, the psychological outlook of the new white immigrants must be contextually juxtaposed with other events. For example, consider the massive land sales perpetrated, and even then being perpetrated, on the original Potawatomi inhabitants. The recent set of treaties—such as the Carey Mission Treaty of 1828 which removed most of the remaining Potawatomi estate from their own control, and the upcoming (and at that time much publically discussed) Chicago Treaty that would be signed in 1833—would usurp the final small tracts of land that they still held.

The Potawatomis' unrest over this land grab resulted in the white pioneers being uneasy and frightened interlopers in Berrien County in 1832. Homesteaders cried for the immediate removal of the Potawatomi to a far-off land called Indian Territory, located west of the Mississippi River (now called Kansas, ironically enough). They clearly feared that the Potawatomi, who had a history of enmity toward first the British and then the Americans, would soon join the Fox tribe and seek a bloody revenge. Now, with the militia on its way, almost the entire fighting force of adult white males would be absent from Berrien County. Thus, there was good reason for a general state of panic. I can remember neither the Black Hawk War nor any allusion to the fact that Berrien County was Potawatomi territory up until the American settlement ever being mentioned in any high-school class. I never even heard the word "Potawatomi" until I was an undergraduate in Ann Arbor, and we were never told when American pioneers first arrived in the county.

This benign approach to our own past ensured that there were never any events over which we must feel shame and remorse. We could thus carry forward our naive morality intact to the next generation. And even if it was not trumpeted by us, we could stand as a silent symbol of what a proper American lifestyle was truly conceived to be. To us was assigned the sacred duty of keeping the country on an even, moral course. Naive indeed!

The Assurance of Recorded History

*B*y the time I graduated from high school in 1958, I had
played twelve basketball games against teams from the
neighboring town of Buchanan. Buchanan was a far larger—Class
B—school system and, as such, their teams were not in our athletic conference. In retrospect, none of the individual games seem
to have been particularly noteworthy. Without the aid of my old
high-school yearbooks, I can recall neither the scores of any of
them nor the team that finally carried that lengthy six-year series.

Only one impression springs unbidden back into my mind.
Overall, these were certainly the twelve worst games of my interscholastic athletic career, beginning when I was in the seventh
grade, because of one Buchanan player who shadowed me closely every game. With unrelenting tenacity, he followed me to the
bench, to the locker room at half-time, and even into the hallway
to the drinking fountain during a time-out. He was constantly at
my elbow, on my back, or in my face.

I don't even remember his name, although I am sure that I must
have known it at the time. But I do know—and this I suddenly realized long after I had graduated and had moved away to Ann
Arbor—that he was a Native American. As far as I know, he was the
only one I ever played against in high school or junior high and the
only one I ever saw, or at least can recognize in my memory, anywhere in Berrien County. As a Native American ethnic, he was
completely invisible. As I was a totally unaware and immature 16-
year-old at that time, this is probably just as well. Any knowledge
of him as a non-white, but definitely non-black or even Hispanic,
person undoubtedly would have thoroughly confused me.

Vaguely I must have known that Native Americans probably
had lived in the vicinity at one time in the far distant past. Yet, how

a Native American had managed to surface in the 1950s in Buchanan would have presented me with one of those imponderable intellectual questions that young people are often beset by while undergoing the intense suffering of maturation. I certainly had no ready academic background to guide me to any satisfactory answer, and I wasn't even aware of a friendly teacher I could turn to for assistance. Thus, I was completely unprepared for the presence of any Native Americans that close to my own hometown.

I had already found out on my own that, when Berrien Springs was first homesteaded beginning in 1829, it was originally called Wolf (sometimes less accurately Wolf's or Wolfe) Prairie. How I chanced onto this sole nugget of information I am not sure. Probably it was from a stray book I happened to browse through in the local town library when I was around 16 years old.

Most of the funding for the Sparks Library came from the Berrien Springs lumber-yard owner Claude R. Sparks. The library was open only three days a week—Tuesday, Thursday, and Saturday—and then for just a few hours. Not many books were housed there. I probably opened most of them at some time or other. Somewhere among them I must have stumbled across one of the few early histories of Berrien County and extracted that single, curious fact which has become lodged in my brain, in a rather worrisome way, for several decades.

One of the more likely candidates for that elusive treatise is Judge Orville W. Coolidge's *A Twentieth Century History of Berrien County, Michigan* (1906). In a short, eight-page section entitled "Oronoko Township," Judge Coolidge informs us that "The present village of Berrien Springs is the site of one of the earliest settlements [1829] made in the township. It was known among the first settlers as Wolf's Prairie, after the name of the Prairie upon which the village is situated." This one small entry in the book is probably all that I read then. I didn't learn why this particular spot of earth was originally called Wolf's Prairie, why the village was named Berrien in 1831, nor why it was rechristened Berrien Springs in 1835. Why, I began to wonder some years later, did it not simply remain Wolf's Prairie? It seems an exotic enough name for a typical Midwestern town, and a far more romantic place to be from.

Two other histories of the region written in the same general era also pass over these events rather cavalierly. Weissert noted tersely in 1900 that in 1831 "Berrien Springs was platted on Wolf's Prairie, and in the first year of its existence a sawmill was erected there." Schwartz [in Ellis], writing some twenty years earlier, is equally laconic, informing us baldly that Berrien Springs is located on a "spot once known as Wolf's Prairie."

One important variation on the name is given in these early attempts at local history. In 1871, Edward B. Cowles refers to it as Wolf Prairie. This is the appellation appearing on the original government survey plat map, and thus it is Wolf Prairie that is considered the more correct version.

Thus, I could gain no solid information as to the derivation of Wolf (or Wolf's) Prairie in these earliest histories of Berrien County—not even any speculation concerning the name, rampant or otherwise. Not until 1924 was an explanation proposed, rather matter-of-factly, by George Fox—a local, and excellent, amateur archeologist and historian. He commented on this confusion between Wolf's and Wolf: "As no settler in the county at this place was named Wolf, it would seem that the latter is the correct designation and was given because of the number of wolves found in this region, according to the pioneers." Although Fox cited no specific statements from pioneers or other primary documents as direct sources for his opinion, this interpretation has become firmly established and cemented into the local tradition. It finally reached the point where, a half a century later, Carney could write in the Berrien County bicentennial volume (1976) concerning the first homestead in Oronoko Township that it was located in what "was known as Wolf's Prairie in those times [1829], a tract of about 1,000 acres where the wolves too frequently howled out their chilling songs of ownership after the sun went down." I must admit that my earliest mental image, upon reading this name for the first time as a teenager around 1956, was one of a pack of wild, snarling, howling wolves with their sharp, pointed canines bared, milling about, presumably seeking a hapless human victim at the top of the steep hill where Ferry Street emerges from the river bottom. I totally discounted the second word in the name (i.e., Prairie).

Any explicit connection between howling wolves and Wolf Prairie can only be inferred since the earliest histories make no direct association between this species of canine animal and this specific 1,000-acre tract of land. In fact, only one reference to wolves is made in all of the Oronoko Township documents. Sometime in the 1830s, according to Schwartz, early settler Henry Freed accidentally chopped his foot with an ax while cutting wood; bleeding heavily, he had to defend himself (or so he related to his friends) from attacks by wolves in order to make his way safely home. Schwartz does list two additional homesteaders in Berrien Township immediately across the St. Joseph River from the present town boundaries who also found the wolves "annoying" in the early 1830s.

In a similar vein, Cowles, writing in 1871 about events that occurred a half a century earlier, commented that in Berrien Township "the wolves were very neighborly and showed a strong inclination to form a closer acquaintance with all the young cattle, sheep or pigs which were not properly cared for by their owner." Wolves and bears were reported to be very "troublesome" by Robert Ferry who homesteaded in Section 27 of Pipestone Township, just north of Berrien Township, in the mid-1830s.

Apparently, not only the first farmers were bothered by these hypothesized wolves. Winslow related that at a time when the mail was still being carried on foot between Niles and St. Joseph, the hapless mail carrier was often caught by night, far from either town, "and had to make his bed in the woods, with no shelter, and his only companions the wolves that made the night hideous by their howlings." Farther to the north in Van Buren County, a bounty was placed on wolves between 1837 and 1848. By the latter date they evidently had been completely eradicated, and the bounty finally was dropped.

Precisely how these various authors came upon their information concerning Berrien County's past wolf population is never made sufficiently clear to me or to any other reader of their tomes. However, by the end of the nineteenth century, as we can see, their prior haunting presence had become well established in the local historical tradition and has continued virtually unabated and unchallenged well into the modern era. Thus, even if no positive correlation can be made between Wolf Prairie and the wolves themselves, some circumstantial evidence does appear to place them in the vicinity of their alleged crimes.

In this regard, it is interesting to note that only three unambiguously identified wolf bones (most likely from the same animal) have been recovered from any of the archeological investigations conducted throughout the county. They derive from the large prehistoric site of Moccasin Bluff which was intermittently occupied for hundreds of years. Most of the county's current resident mammals are present in the faunal collections at Moccasin Bluff and are known from several other local sites, particularly from those situated along the St. Joseph River just north of Berrien

Springs. Both finely cut wolf mandibles and maxillas were impor- tant ritual paraphernalia for Native Americans, and the near absence of faunal remains of this species in the local archeological record is quite surprising. Also included in these samples of ani- mal remains are several additional mammals such as black bear and mountain lion that are absent from the county today, and the coyote that is only lately reentering the local ecosystem.

The coyote is a particularly fascinating creature. In his *Gazetter of the State of Michigan* (1838), John T. Blois writes con- cerning the state's animal species: "There are three kinds of wolves, the *canis lupus*, or gray wolf; the *canis latrans*, or prairie wolf; and the *canis lycaon*, or large black wolf, all of which, in the opinion of our farmers and first settlers, are too plenty for con- venience. The little prairie wolf is the most mischievous of all." *Canis latrans*, Blois' prairie wolf, is known today as the coyote. Thus, coyotes were seemingly misidentified as wolves by many of the earliest observers.

With these observations in mind, it becomes entirely credible that coyotes, which the archeological data also say were most like- ly quite common in the region before A.D. 1600, later had been structurally transformed by the early white settlers into the much more romantic (and dangerous) species of wolves. As a result, this rememorization process would have increased the latter's pre- sumed population size and would have allowed them to enter quite gracefully and inexorably into their current legendary status.

Other circumstantial evidence provides us with a lead to an entirely different interpretation. In 1983 Erwin Stuntz privately published a volume entitled *The Incredible Wheel of Time*. This book is a truly massive and unsystematic compilation of his historical and archeological observations concerning the Native Americans of northern Indiana and southwestern Michigan. At one point in the book, he guides us up the St. Joseph River while he points out the locations of former Indian villages. Under the section "Oronoko Township," he makes this comment:

> Chief Wolf Maria's village is upstream on the west side of the St. Joseph River settled in the hills in Sec. 13, 18 [sic], and 24, now Main Street in Berrian [sic] Springs. This was a large village with one burial ground where Main Street in [sic] now on the hill near the U.S. 31 River Bridge.... There was a fair-sized burial site in Sec. 24 in the southeast part of town, proving that many Indians lived here for many years.

Stuntz, too, provides neither primary archeological nor ethnohistoric documentation for any of his bold assertions; but his opinions, based upon many years of personal field and library investigations, are certainly worth pursuing farther.

Only two of the initial local historians specifically attempted to correlate Wolf Prairie with a prewhite contact occupation of Native Americans. Cowles remarked in 1871 that "It is the general opinion of the earlier settlers that the prairie was once covered with a forest, which was destroyed by a wind storm, and that the ground was cleared and cultivated by Indians. Indications of former corn fields were plainly visible when the first settlers came." Further, Turner, in his *Gazetteer* (1867) which likewise is replete with anonymous quotes, refers to the probable remains of an Indian village within the present town limits itself: "the beautifully embowered Indian Fields [the Grove today], still retaining the footmarks of barbaric life." Hence, the Cowles and Turner documents locate an Indian occupation on Wolf Prairie prior to the initial white settlement.

In 1828, E. (Ebenezer) Reed, a Michigan Territorial official, dispatched a series of letters to Governor Lewis Cass concerning the Native American population along the St. Joseph River, an area that would eventually become Berrien County after statehood had been attained. By this date, the major Native American villages along the river, most of which were located near present-day Niles, were populated largely with Potawatomis (although they were often mixed with residents who were members of other tribes). Reed was collecting as much background information as possible for Governor Cass who was busily preparing for the upcoming Carey Mission Treaty of September 20, 1828. This treaty would result in the Potawatomis ceding much of their remaining ancestral land to the Territory of Michigan.

Reed also compiled an extremely poor map for Cass, one lacking any scale and paying little attention to the specific details of the river's meandering pattern. However, a short distance downriver from Moccasin's village at Moccasin Bluff, which is just north of present-day Buchanan, he placed a series of four huts (symbols of separate villages or of individual houses?), one of which he referred to as Big Wolf's. He described Big Wolf as "a very respectable Indian, said to be the best hunter in the tribe. He is allowed to have some influence, but is no speaker." This is our sole description of Big Wolf, probably the earliest settler of Wolf Prairie for whom we have a name. Reed's map, and his brief rendering of a Potawatomi individual named Chief Big Wolf, situate a village under his leadership near the soon-to-be-platted town of Berrien Springs in 1828. So the original name of Wolf Prairie most likely derives not from the dreaded, fearsome *Canis lupus* but from a Native American, Big Wolf, a Potawatomi who would be quickly removed from the new town's collective memory.

The map and accompanying brochure, *Historic Sites of Berrien County, Michigan*, published by the Berrien Community Foundation, Inc., in 1989, recognizes but hastily skims over this connection. The author of the brochure noted simply that "Wolf's Prairie [was] the former hunting grounds of Chief Big Wolf." One has the distinct impression that Big Wolf merely wandered randomly through the future—but not yet constructed or even platted—town of Berrien Springs as his stomach demanded. Nowhere is it considered that he might have actually settled there with several families of his clan in a permanent village. That he might have had a stake in the land itself is not deemed a possibility.

John Pike, after sojourning at the Carey Mission near Niles in 1829, moved with his family to a homestead at Wolf Prairie. All of the local histories mistakenly award Pike, and not Big Wolf or probably much more accurately an earlier Native American, the honorary role of First Citizen. Even before platting was begun around Wolf Prairie in 1829, according to the initial plat map, a Lawrence Cavanaugh had already constructed a small house and had planted twenty acres of corn in a field that now straddles what would become designated by government surveyors as Sections 25 and 26.

Pike and his family were accompanied to their new homestead by Pitt Brown's nephew Horace Godfrey. Pike and Godfrey were followed ten days later by George Kimmel who would establish a permanent residence on a 300-acre homestead in 1831. Before his death in 1849, Kimmel eventually possessed around 10,000 acres of land in the vicinity of the newly established town.

Jacob Shoemaker, who had arrived along with Kimmel, quickly purchased two acres in Indian Fields. One of Kimmel's daughters later married another new settler, Francis Murdock, who took possession of 120 acres of Wolf Prairie. Their daughter Eliza, in October of 1831, was the first white child born in the new village. (In 1832, a Captain Wilson was the initial white American to be buried in Indian Fields.) These freshly settled families were joined by Pitt Brown in 1831. Brown operated Berrien Springs' first hotel which was situated on the west bank of the St. Joseph River along with a distillery and a ferry service across the river—both presumably necessary enterprises. He was also the village's first postmaster, for the post office was located in the tavern of his hotel.

Berrien County was officially organized on March 4, 1831. Later that same year, the village of Berrien was platted by surveyor Samuel Mars at the request of Brown, Godfrey, and Murdock. Four years later the name was changed to Berrien Springs. Berrien, the term given to both the new village and the county, derives from John M. Berrien, a former senator from the state of Georgia who was at that time the Attorney General in President Andrew Jackson's cabinet (1829-1831). For completeness, we again cite Turner from one of his unattributed sources: The town has "a fine chalybeate [iron] spring within the corporation, and a sulphur spring on the opposite side of the river." Thus, we have our new name of Berrien Springs.

But why wasn't "Wolf Prairie" acceptable to the new settlers? The answer to this particular question requires us to adopt another perspective. With the symbolic action of renaming, the white settlers had taken final possession of Wolf Prairie. This newly applied label was not merely the ultimate act of seizure of the land itself. It also signified a successful erasure of the Native Americans' own unwritten and, hence, seemingly mythical past—one that had belonged uniquely to this 1,000-acre plot of ground. Wolf Prairie and its Native American heritage had now ceased to exist in the minds of its new inhabitants. The conquest was now complete.

In their place, later writers of local history would one day commemorate an American carnivore (which itself already possessed a long mythical past)—one that required another generation of intensive effort to eradicate it from the rapidly changing landscape of Southwestern Michigan. First the Native Americans and then the wolves, both symbols of a wild, savage, uncivilized, and, therefore, clearly nonwhite world, would shrink from active memory. They ultimately disappeared into invisibility in the ensuing rush for settlement. Wolf Prairie could at last be successfully tamed, and the true history of Berrien Springs, as the migrating Americans and immigrating Europeans understood the concept, could safely begin. In this new culture, they demanded, the past would henceforth be narrated as history and not as mythology.

Across the Field

---

*B*y the time I was growing up in the mid-1950s, no vestiges
remained of the now vanquished Wolf Prairie—neither
the unique species of flora and fauna that had once flourished
there nor their images that could linger only in the town's collective memory. I never once heard the name of "Wolf Prairie"
uttered aloud by a single resident of my home village. I don't
remember it being mentioned, even in the briefest of passages, in
the *Journal Era*. Without Coolidge's small subchapter on Oronoko
Township, I would have been completely unaware that a significant 1,000-acre prairie had formerly occupied the space where the
town of Berrien Springs now stands.

I have an aerial photograph of Oronoko Township on my lab-
oratory worktable. It was taken in the late 1970s and was published by the United States Department of Agriculture. It accom-
panies a comprehensive soil survey of Berrien County. No outline
of Wolf Prairie is emblazoned in black marker across this photo.
Where wild grasses once thrived with their roots deeply embedded and intricately entwined within the rich prairie earth, today
one finds only concrete streets, stores, houses, yards, gardens, and
vacant lots on which we once played countless games of baseball
in the hot summer sun.

One unidentified, but apparently original, settler of the town
informed Franklin Ellis around the year 1880 that in 1832 "the
prairie grass upon what is now the village of Berrien Springs was
as high as a man's head." Today, one can hope to recover this
nearly forgotten and invisible landscape only through the environmental reconstructions created by natural scientists who hold
an abiding interest in the land's past. We can bring back this once
dynamic ecosystem only as a series of shadowy images, never

again whole and in constant movement with the wind and water. Now that image only flickers dimly across our minds.

The most complete recreation of Wolf Prairie was prepared by paleobotanist Bert C. Ebbers in conjunction with the US-31 Berrien County Freeway Archaeological Project during the 1980s. The overall research undertaking was directed by Dr. Elizabeth B. Garland of Western Michigan University (no relation to the Garlands of Berrien Springs).

When the earliest French explorers came to the area in the late seventeenth century, they found that the dissected morainal uplands and valley bottoms of Berrien County supported a vast diversity of plant communities. These ranged from flood plains, swamp forests, and other wetlands (including tamarack swamps and wet prairies) to mesic (moderately moist) beech-sugar maple climax forests and open, oak savannas and dry prairies. Wolf Prairie, at 1,000 or so acres in overall size, was the largest of the three dry prairies then existing in the county. The other two were Portage Prairie just south of Niles and Terre Coupe Prairie to the southwest near the town of Galien. Wolf Prairie was an isolated, eastern outlier of the Prairie Peninsula, that northeastern rim of generally open, virtually treeless landscape that extended south-westwardly from southern Michigan to where it finally sub-merged gently into the North American Great Plains.

Nowhere is the local environment adequately described either by the earliest European (French) visitors or by the American pioneers in the township. We can read tantalizing bits and pieces about the St. Joseph River, about the dark, massive, and forbidding fringing forests, and about murky, fetid backswamps. These early explorers and the later homesteaders were intently focused on other interests—most acutely on problems of daily survival in this new and largely alien world. They certainly were not concerned with the aesthetics of the region's natural beauty.

Therefore, only hints of the original Oronoko countryside remained. At the time of initial white-American settlement, much of what we know today about the area's ecosystem in the early nineteenth century derives almost entirely by accident from evidence gathered by the United States government-mandated surveys conducted in the county by the General Land Office from 1827 to 1831. Inadvertently, the resultant survey maps and surveyors' notebooks recorded isolated bits of vegetation data for posterity.

These professional surveyors, including Lucius Lyon, marked two "witness trees" with blazes to delineate the corner boundaries of the sections of public land that were being made available for homesteading. These six-mile-square geometric sections were the harbingers of the civilization for which the surveyors were rapidly and inexorably preparing the land. They believed that their blazes would continually remain because, "surely, these endless forests and their majestic trees will abide on this land forever."

The surveyors carefully recorded the species of their individual witness trees, their approximate overall size, and the exact location of one or two additional trees that intersected their ever straight, never swerving survey lines. A typical day-book entry by surveyor William Brookfield in 1829 reads as follows: "Enter Wolf Prairie. Set P. corner to sect. 13 & 24. W Oak 22 S14 W5.20.... Land rolling & 1st rate. Timber B and W Oak Beech & Whitewood." These survey maps and the accompanying notebooks with the surveyors' terse entries, nonetheless, permit distribution maps of the major vegetation types and their supporting ecosystems over much of the former Northwest Territory to be plotted with some fair degree of accuracy. A hazy, indistinct picture of the land's past slowly begins to emerge.

The ground layer of Wolf Prairie appears to have been dominated by various species of composite plants. Two grasses, big bluestem and little bluestem, were the most significant. The upperstory deciduous trees, according to the surveyors' accounts, included white oak, hickory, and ash. Hazelnut trees bordered the prairie. Hickory and hazelnut trees both provided edible fruits in addition to the wild strawberries, raspberries, and various other types of berries adapted to open prairie environments.

Large game animals, particularly the white-tailed deer and the larger American elk, respond well to this mosaic type of ecosystem. They feed heavily on the woody plants not available to them in denser, closed-canopy forests. Beyond offering abundant food, the oak savanna also provides shelter from predators, including humans. Further, when these savannas and prairies are regularly burned over, whether from natural lightning-strike fires or from inevitable human carelessness, new plant growth, particularly the brushy berry species and the grassy forage, immediately follow. These wildfires maintain the rich prairie grasses and shrubs since they burn off the smaller tree seedlings and encourage rapid regeneration of seedy plants and root suckers that compete for the limited space. Thus, a continuous supply of fresh browse and seeds is provided for the local resident mammal populations.

In order to accomplish this archeological project, one must understand the succession of prehistoric environments in the county. Palynologists Phyliss J. Ahearn and Ronald O. Kapp extracted extensive pollen cores from three separate localities. These cores allow us to reconstruct the long, but always changing, vegetational history of the immediate vicinity of the St. Joseph River. It is one that extends back into the late Ice Age when the last glacier completed its final, grinding, melting recession from Berrien County.

One of the cores was drawn from a sphagnum bog located on the Froehlich farm across the river to the northeast of the town. From here we learn that, with the disappearance of the last (or Wisconsin) ice sheet, the barren landscape was invaded quickly by trees that included coniferous spruce-fir and pines along with a few species of hardwoods. This phase was followed rapidly by deciduous trees which came to dominate the forest composition, black ash being the most important of those growing in and along the alder-willow swamps existing near the river.

Up until about 5,500 years ago, the Froehlich basin was covered by an open lake bordered by oaks, elms, beech, and basswood trees. Then beech, aspen, and cottonwood began to increase at the expense of oak and basswood. Pollen analysts also record the presence of ragweed, amaranth, chenopodium, and various other species of weedy grasses. This section of the spectrum indicates both a distinctly warming climatic trend and the presence of open, prairie-like areas in the immediate proximity of the lake.

A second core from this date, taken from a point bar on an old terrace on the Wymer property—which is about one mile to the southeast of the Froelich Bog and just west of the St. Joseph River—confirms the existence of a beech-dominated, hardwood forest interspersed with extensive meadow openings. Between 5,000 and 2,400 years ago, the distribution of oak trees again greatly expanded; finally, around 2,400 years ago, the modern mixed beech/maple forest of today appeared. Still we must not think that climatic stability had been attained. The pollen record shows several minor and rapid fluctuations of moister and drier periods alternating across this temporal span of more than two millennia.

The vegetation zones along the river were conditioned not only by long-term weather cycles but also by variations in the water regimes of the river which themselves were tied, in turn, to changes in the surface levels of Lake Michigan. Major fluctuations in lake-level elevations are seen from the beginning of the glacial retreat when large amounts of water were suddenly released by melting ice and the Lake Michigan Basin finally became liberated. Following the onset of glacial retreat, these variations continued over the next several thousand years as once-active outlet channels of the post glacial lakes were abandoned, new ones were created, and the land itself rebounded (uplifted) from the massive weight of the ice cover from which it was now freed.

Some 5,000 years ago, the surface level of Lake Michigan stood more than 20 feet higher than it does today. Thus, the low-lying river bottom land around Berrien Springs would have been permanently flooded. Much of the drier, fertile soils near the river today would have been covered by marshes and wetlands. This process is still going on. The historic record from 1830 to 1983 shows fluctuations of approximately 6 feet in the mean sea level of Lake Michigan.

Faunal data from the U.S.-31 archeological project also provide valuable insights into the numbers of species and the distribution of mammals in the region prior to white contact. The Rock Hearth archeological site, on the present Andrews University property, yielded evidence of large quantities of elk, white tailed-deer, beaver, and muskrats from contexts dating between 1,000 and 2,000 B.C. A similar faunal composition was recovered at the nearby and slightly later (ca. 1,000 B.C.) Wymer site. Upriver at Moccasin Bluff, these same mammals, along with black bear, rabbit, porcupine, wolf, coyote, fox, otter, and squirrel, are recorded during the early second millennium A.D. With the exception of the coyote, these are the same larger animals that are mentioned most frequently in the early local history volumes.

Another source of information is the day books of fur trader William Burnett. Burnett, whose post was situated near present-day St. Joseph, was born in New Jersey. After migrating to south-western Michigan just prior to 1780, he married Kawkemee, sister of Topinabee who was one of the major leaders of the Potawatomi. Burnett's day book records the number of furs by specific animal that he purchased from local Native Americans in his trading activities. Some of these data, focusing directly on the major fur-bearing mammals, are given in the table on page 32.

The table shows the rapid depletion within less than a single decade of all of these fur-bearing mammals from the lower reaches of the St. Joseph River watershed. Clearly, a large-scale catas-

ANIMAL	1796/97	1800/01
Beaver	117	9
Fisher	97	0
Muskrat	5091	1076
Bear	160	10
Fox	280	107
Mink	517	248
Otter	436	119
Raccoon	22,032	5603

Major fur-bearing mammals with the number of furs William Burnett purchased from the Native Americans.

trophe was responsible for the removal of these species from the local environment. Locally, black bears and wild turkeys were nearly extinct by the middle of the nineteenth century. In the 1950s, the imported pheasant had replaced the indigenous wild turkey, and only the muskrats and raccoons survived in any quantity. I rarely saw a red fox or a white-tailed deer as a boy. The other species listed in the table were absent in the 1950s, completely forgotten as once having graced the county's landscape.

Thus, when Euro-Americans began their initial migration into the upper reaches of the St. Joseph River Valley, they found an intricate mosaic of plant and animal communities, varying from bluff top and moraine crest to marshy river bottom. But it was a dynamic, living ecosystem marked by a unique historical past. For me, as a boy, however, it was simply a vast playground to explore, one of infinite nooks and crannies and countless natural treasures.

The present-day Grove is located along the bluff top at the south end of South Main Street and adjacent to the former Wolf Prairie. In 1833, George Kimmel purchased much of the property at a government-land sale held in White Pigeon Prairie as part of his ultimate 10,000 acres. Kimmel sold the section of land that later become known as the Grove to Samuel Townsend and Peter Seton Harvey in 1836. In 1870, Dr. Lyman Barnard took control of a parcel of Wolf Prairie from descendants of the Townsends and "improved" it by clearing off the accumulated secondary growth of brush, weeds, and young trees that were inexorably reclaiming the land since the time of its last cultivation. The results of this natural process of revegetation was regarded as merely an eyesore by the townspeople.

Dr. Barnard was one of the original organizers of the Pioneer

The Grove circa 1920 on property originally owned by George Kimmel.

Association of Berrien County with a membership consisting of pre-1851 homesteaders; their annual meeting at the Grove came to be called Old Settler's Day. This eagerly anticipated event reportedly drew thousands of participants. Beginning in 1877, the Grove also served as a recreation area for the Young People's Picnic Association of Berrien County, and their ceremonial affairs were also heavily attended. Both of these associations were long since defunct (and completely forgotten?) by the mid-twentieth century, and I was completely unfamiliar with them.

The plot of ground was officially designated as a town park in 1881, the land having been purchased by the village from the Platt family for $922.90. Numerous local events were held there, including a whirlwind visit by the Reverend Billy Sunday who preached to 4,000 eager listeners on Old Settlers' Day, June 11, 1913. A large pavilion was constructed in 1916, and subsequent holiday rituals drew avid participants from as far away as Chicago and South Bend. In 1946, the Grove served as the first Berrien County Youth Fair Grounds.

By the early 1950s, the former Indian Fields was quiescent. For my friends and me, the Grove was a place for war games and endless rounds of Cowboys and Indians. Its heavily timbered landscape provided hide-outs and seemingly unlimited locations for springing ambushes on the unwary. At night, particularly in the summer, it also functioned as a trysting place for lovers. Couples would park in cars along the rutted dirt roadways criss-crossing the Grove, and we would take them by surprise. Shining our flashlights on them, we often had the good luck of discovering them—arms and legs entangled—in totally compromising positions. Then we would flee in haste, howling over our shoulders with mocking laughter.

One moonless autumn night, Dave Loss and I were ambushed ourselves by a carload of angry young males whom we had surprised once too often. They chased us through the thickly treed landscape with mayhem on their minds while we fled in haste, and, I must admit, abject fear. We escaped unharmed and, fortunately, unrecognized since our feet could find the familiar paths even where there was no light for us to see. Behind us, we could hear them thudding dully into trees in the dark. The next morning at school, one senior showed up with a beautiful black eye that he claimed he had received in a fight with a kid from New Troy. For once, discretion kept us from loudly proclaiming the truth.

But the Grove in which we roamed and played so rapaciously was not a remnant of the natural pre-settlement woods. Those earlier trees had been felled so that the light of civilization could strike the forest floor. Among the first industries in the newly platted town, as Weissert informs us, were the sawmills built by George Kimmel and Pitt Brown in 1831. Into whatever wilderness these pioneers ventured, the dense, extensive forests were considered impediment to the large-scale agriculture so necessary for a growing population. In the typical American-pioneer fashion, they were rapidly cut down. In the phrasing of Nettie Ferrell, author of an article entitled "Berrien Springs History" (*Journal Era*, June 20, 1956), "subduing the forest" was a primary endeavor. Wolf Prairie was swiftly bared by the surrounding open spaces of the new village of Berrien Springs.

In the town, as with so many like it across the country once the great forests disappeared, the trees were then replanted—oaks, maples, and elms lined the concrete sidewalks of my youth. My great grandmother's house, situated as it was on the corner, was enclosed on two street sides by nine towering maple trees that provided continuous summer shade and a riot of fall colors and afternoon raking. In the autumn we lined piles of leaves for more than 200 feet along the streets and, with rapt fascination, we trailed slowly and totally absorbed alongside the fire and smoke as it consumed the summer's past glory.

It was here, then, in today's cut-over, second-growth woods at the south end of town, that the Big Wolf village was most probably situated. Quite possibly the same river bluff had witnessed even earlier Native American settlements. The 1870s homesteaders who—according to Cowles—had recognized a Native American presence prior to their own arrival had that much correct, even if they were unable to recall the chief's name (had they ever really known it?). However, when they offered the opinion that a violent wind storm had been responsible for originally opening the fields that the Native Americans subsequently cultivated until a large and conspicuous prairie had been created, they were quite clearly wrong.

Prairies, in general, were not new to Berrien County. Wolf Prairie had already had a long-standing existence well before its soils were disturbed by human cultivators. The location for the new village was carefully selected by Big Wolf and the Potawatomi. It afforded rapid access to the water and fish of the St. Joseph River as well as to the fertile and easily worked soils and other life-giving resources, both plant and animal, that frequented the adjoining woodlands, meadows, and swamps.

With the merger of the town and the unobstructed space around it, Wolf Prairie disappeared physically. And it was also removed from the village's memory. Indian Fields now became simply a name without its own proper history. In 1956, only the heavily wooded Grove remained, the very polar opposite of the open prairie of the year 1829.

A People Without History

M any, when they are teenagers, already know exactly what they will do with their lives. Such was the case with most of my friends who were busily preparing to be farmers or housewives. In school, they were dutiful members of the Future Farmers of America or the Future Homemakers of America, and Shop and Homemaking were heavily enrolled and (frequently) attended classes. (In 1956, the 4-H was the largest voluntary youth organization in the world.) Several of my male classmates would more formally hone their nascent agricultural skills at Michigan State University. A few of my peers were aiming toward teaching careers and would go on to study secondary education at Western Michigan in Kalamazoo. Luckily, I did not have to carry around the burden of commitment to a particular career. Thus, I was allowed to seek out and eventually find another very different kind of future. I settled for curiosity rather than for security. Nonetheless, anthropology was a life's work that I came upon quite by accident.

The aptitude tests that all students must grind through, and extensive counseling with Victor King, our high-school advisor, always and inevitably pushed me toward engineering. I diligently studied college brochures from technical institutes, read books on engineering, and even entered the University of Michigan—where no one from my home town had matriculated, at least for many years—as a probable mathematics major. However, despite the welcome encouragement I received, these possible futures held virtually no interest for me.

In high school I had never even heard the word "anthropology." We had some odd form of social studies, but, in the 1950s, these courses focused quite pointedly on modern economics and a kind of basic, white-male American sociology. What might have sparked an early passion was there before me on and in the earth, but it remained completely invisible to my eyes.

One day, for example, I was pheasant hunting just downriver from Moccasin Bluff with Kenny "Stork" Schauber, his brother Charlie, and his future brother-in-law Denny Baab. I did not know then that this was an important Native American archeological site which had been excavated in 1948 and that it contained occupations predating the European discovery of the New World. My sole knowledge was simply that Moccasin, because of the apparent peculiarity of his name, had most likely been an American Indian. We chanced across a partially filled-in and abandoned cellar in a stand of scrub growth. Charlie began rooting around in the fill, asking questions such as "Who lived here?" and "Why did they leave?" I fervently began urging that we continue the excursion after birds, but Charlie gave me a sort of "How can you not find this hole in the ground interesting?" glare. Frankly, I did not; I was totally unprepared for any acknowledgment of the past.

Over the last 30 years, I have read countless archeological site reports, many of them dealing explicitly with the prehistory of Southwestern Michigan. I am struck now by how many of these ancient sites are found near Berrien Springs and abut the St. Joseph River. I had walked over most of them during my youth while hunting or hiking. Yet, I never saw a single artifact lying on the ground despite the fact that I kept my eyes constantly glued there searching for any animal signs. Certainly, even then, I could have recognized an ancient arrowhead, although shards from a broken pottery vessel, a flint scraping tool, or a ceremonial gorget might have been far too exotic for my teenage comprehension.

Beyond Moccasin Bluff, the only other reference I remember, and only vaguely at that, is a connection between Sumnerville, just over the boundary line into Cass County, and "Indians." My original source to this connection was my mother, and it was probably sometime in the late 1940s. As we drove past the single large building that constituted the commercial portion of that little settlement that was barely more than a wide spot on the road, she mentioned that some Indians had lived there once. From that time on, I could never drive through Sumnerville on that winding back-country road without my brain shouting "Indians" to me.

But beyond that single occasion, I possessed no additional information concerning any community of Native Americans who had actually resided there or were currently present anywhere in southwestern Michigan.

Although I vaguely knew of a Potawatomi settlement in historic times in Sumnerville, I first learned something concrete about the Native American presence in and around Sumnerville only after beginning my studies in anthropology at Ann Arbor in the early 1960s. A major cluster of burial mounds found in Sumnerville had been dated back some fifteen hundred or so years. Most of the physical evidence had largely disappeared by then, but some of the archeological data had been published in the 1930s. Unfortunately, the current village powers had posted no marker to draw attention to its unique past.

Except for the Moccasin Bluff site, professional archeological interest in the prehistory of Berrien County had not, by 1956, been particularly enthusiastic. Quite a number of amateurs, however, had collected and excavated several locations throughout the region. As high-school students, we were never made aware of the existence of these individuals, even though one of them, Amos Green, lived in Eau Claire, not too far from Berrien Springs. It was these original labors, including those of Joe Birdsell of South Bend who conducted the initial work at Moccasin Bluff and who donated extensive artifact collections to the University of Michigan, that eventually sparked more intensive field investigations. Any understanding that we have today of the Native Americans' past in Berrien County owes much to them and the thousands of unpaid hours that these avocational archeologists contributed simply out of love for their home territory and its abiding, intriguing mysteries.

Native Americans first entered southwestern Michigan shortly after the final wasting of the last glacial ice from the region. Lanceolate-shaped spear points with a basal flute or channel that date back several millennia are numerous throughout the county. They are frequently associated with fossil-lake beaches, both those of the former, and higher, shorelines of Lake Michigan and of large inland bodies of water that are now extinct. One of the latter was glacial Lake Dowagiac, which was fed by melting ice. It generally followed the course of the present-day Dowagiac River except that it extended all the way to what is now the Kankakee River in northern Indiana. Some of these fossil beaches are still clearly visible.

Mammoths and mastodons roamed the landscape. The Prillwitz mammoth found and unearthed in 1962 in Berrien Township, and reported in the *Michigan Archaeologist* by Amos Green, apparently lived while Native Americans were already resident in the area. It is not certain whether or not they feasted off of this particular animal, but no clear evidence shows that they were responsible for its demise.

With the final wasting of the ice sheet, there directly followed a large-scale extinction of the larger mammals such as mammoths and mastodons as well as a general retreat northward of such animals as the caribou and musk oxen. Native Americans began to concentrate their annual resource exploitation on the diverse and far more predictable—and hence more reliable—wild plants and smaller mammals, fish, and shellfish that inhabited the extensive inland lakes and wetlands dotting the new and rapidly evolving postglacial landscape. This hunting and gathering adaptation greatly intensified, eventually reaching a high point beginning around 1000 B.C.

Native Americans, by this date, were trading widely for non-local raw materials such as flints and participating in intercultural relationships with peoples in northern Michigan and the Saginaw region, east/central Ohio, and eastern Illinois. The St. Joseph River formed a conduit eastward and also westward along the Kankakee into the Illinois River Valley. Small amounts of copper started reaching the area from the massive sources located in the Lake Superior region.

Many of the archeological sites discovered and excavated by Dr. Garland date within the period of ca. 2000 B.C. to A.D. 300. Native Americans were heavily exploiting the extensive local varieties of nuts, tubers, berries, and seedy wild grasses, the remains of many of which have been recovered from sites excavated in the U.S. 31 right-of-way on the Edison, Stover, and Wymer properties. Animal bones, because they are often destroyed by the local acidic soils, were rare; but they did include deer, elk, squirrel, muskrat, and beaver. The taking of various fish, such as lake sturgeon, along with several species of turtles and mussels, produced important seasonal foods. Most surprising, however, was the finding of some domesticated sunflower seeds, clearly showing that Native Americans in Berrien County were practicing a small-scale horticulture most likely along the mud flats of the river by ca. 1010 B.C.

At the Rock Hearth site, archeologists recovered the outlines of a U-shaped hut structure dating to approximately 1800 B.C. Also excavated from the site were several dozen storage and refuse pits which contained evidence of the Native American subsistence activities. Deer and elk remains were plentiful along with lesser amounts of beaver and muskrat. The inhabitants also collected and then processed large quantities of walnuts, hickory nuts, and butternuts. Rock Hearth appears to have been occupied during the summer and fall seasons. During the spring the site, sitting as it does on the modern flood plain, would have been under water.

A single Native American burial of an adult male from this time period was discovered by George Kimmel on his property in 1958. The individual appeared to have been wearing a necklace made of copper beads and a copper gorget with two holes drilled in it for suspension. He also had had a copper crescent placed on his chest at the time of his interment. Cached near his place of burial, but not directly in association with his grave, were 450 sub-triangular bifacially chipped flint blades and four chert projectile points shaped like Turkey tails.

Two additional caches of more than 125 of these subtriangular flint blades have been found buried elsewhere along the St. Joseph River bluffs. Thirty-four large turkey-tail points were also recovered on the Conrad farm to the south in Bertrand Township. Finally, other probable ceremonial objects, including two sandal-sole-shaped gorgets of slate and a banner stone, were picked up off the surface of a major, but not excavated, site located in the nearby Galien River basin.

Shortly before the beginning of the Christian era, Berrien County seems to have lain at the interface of two emerging and widespread burial cults: the Red Ochre (signified by the flint cache blades and turkey tails) and the Glacial Kame (the sandal-sole gorgets). Neither burial cult is well understood by archeologists even today. The first synthetic study of the Glacial Kame burials was published in 1948 by Wilbur Cunningham, a Benton Harbor lawyer who collected what data were still available from the sites—most already destroyed by then from gravel mining—located in southern Michigan and northern Indiana and Ohio. This culture featured massive interments (often more than one hundred burials) in the natural gravel kame hills left behind thousands of years earlier by the retreating ice. They honored some of their dead with the inclusion of sandal-sole-shaped gorgets, usually manufactured from marine shells imported from the Florida Gulf Coast. Because of my interest in his 1948 study, I went to visit Mr. Cunningham in his office in 1962. By that time, he seemed to have lost all interest in Glacial Kame and kept redirecting our conversation to his recent book *Land of Four Flags*, a very readable history of Berrien County. I left his office disappointed; unfortunately for me, this was the only time that I ever had the opportunity to talk with him.

By the end of this temporal interval (around 1000 B.C.), large burial-mound complexes had begun appearing in the Upper Ohio River drainage, the Illinois Valley, and their environs. One, the Norton Mound Group, was located near Grand Rapids, and several are known from along the Muskegon River. Sumnerville was the local participant in this widespread type of burial ceremonialism. Decorations etched into the wet clay of their ceramics before firing and the presence in graves of exotic, nonlocal flints show that the people at Sumnerville were in contact with other groups from both the Illinois Valley and the Saginaw area.

Twelve burial mounds, a horseshoe-shaped ditch, two ossuaries (mass burials in a single grave), and a ceremonial-pit feature are known from Sumnerville. Nine of these burial mounds were first recorded by William Brookfield in his initial Government Land Office Survey. (Brookfield also surveyed in Oronoko Township.) Six of the mounds are still visible today, one of which has an oak tree perhaps 200 years old growing out of one of its sides. In 1967, after Jim Fitting, then an archeologist at the University of Michigan, and I had examined the Conrad Turkey Tail cache, we briefly visited the Sumnerville site. This time I saw Sumnerville with new eyes.

Excavations by Garland at Sumnerville in the 1980s recovered seven bundle burials in Ossuary 1 and the remains of at least 12 individuals in Ossuary 2. Surprising was a pit that contained no formal burials but did yield a clay ceramic vessel, a blade of white chert (possibly from an Illinois source), a broken blue-gray slate gorget, and several human teeth lacking an associated jaw bone. The human teeth had apparently been placed in a leather or fabric bag. The clay vessel, along with about twelve litres of red ochre, was laid over the artifacts. A radiocarbon date places the event around A.D. 300. Ossuary 1 dates to about A.D. 600. Sumnerville, thus, functioned as a major cemetery for Native Americans for perhaps more than half a millennium.

True agricultural villages such as those described by the French in the seventeenth century make their appearance only after A.D. 1000. Extensive excavations at Moccasin Bluff and surface collections of artifacts from many parts of the county demonstrate the continuing importance of the St. Joseph River not only as a source of wild foods and as a lifeline for transportation but also for the rich valley-bottom soils for corn, beans, and squash horticulture. These villages signal that a new way of life had begun for Native Americans in this region.

Moccasin Bluff was occupied intermittently long before Chief Moccasin situated his group there and even well prior to the appearance of corn agriculture. Evidence of two prehistoric agricultural settlements was found: one dating about A.D. 1200 and another dating around A.D. 1550 or approximately one century before the French arrived in Berrien County. The site provides an opportunity to glimpse, albeit imperfectly, a local Native American lifestyle just prior to historic contact.

Corn cob remains were plentiful from pits on the site, showing that these new agricultural techniques were capable of satisfying a large part of the plant diet. Indeed, these techniques appear to have been successful enough so that the local extensive nut crops seem to have been mostly ignored. Meat was derived heavily from deer, elk, and lake sturgeon. Nearly 75 percent of the meat eaten at Moccasin Bluff apparently came from deer and elk.

Some 46.7 percent of the animal bones were identified as deriving from a single species of fish, the sturgeon. Adult sturgeon average about 60 pounds in weight and 100-pound fish are common. They swim upriver from Lake Michigan to spawn in the spring when the water temperature rises to between 57 and 60°F. There they could be netted easily or speared in shallow water. Moccasin Bluff is situated along a riffle pattern in the channel of the St. Joseph River, rendering it ideal for the capture of large numbers of fish under shallow water conditions.

Stone and clay pipes were found on the site; smoking was both an everyday practice and, undoubtedly, a significant part of most ceremonies. In historic times, many Native Americans used turtle carapaces as tobacco trays; several carapaces were recovered on the site. Copper was rare, and marine shell was absent. Most of their trade outside the area was for flint for tool manufacture rather than for the exotic raw materials destined for ceremonial objects seen in earlier eras.

Moccasin Bluff was occupied year-round. The ceramics from the site feature clam-shell tempering and design elements indicating that the inhabitants had extensive contacts with similar settlements extending northward to the Muskegon River and southward around Lake Michigan to the Chicago region. Some of the pipe styles suggest interaction with Native Americans along the Little Miami River near Cincinnati.

The ethnic identity of the Bluff inhabitants is somewhat controversial. Robert Bettarel, who published the results of the excavations in 1973 and who was my colleague in graduate school, suggested that the Moccasin Bluff inhabitants were probably the Miami. Most researchers, however, have opted for the Potawatomi. Both tribal groups were present along the St. Joseph River by the end of the seventeenth century, and either one may have been resident prior to French contact.

Outside of Moccasin Bluff, additional sites dating from the last few centuries prior to French contact seem to be rare in Berrien County. Only four are known in the Galien River Basin and a couple have been recorded in Oronoko Township. The latter have been test-excavated, but the results as yet have not been published. We are uncertain whether or not Indian Fields was occupied before Big Wolf arrived with his families of Potawatomi as no excavations have ever been conducted there, at least any from which the data have been made available. It is most likely that Indian Fields witnessed habitation prior to Big Wolf.

By the early seventeenth century, Berrien County had been abandoned by its resident Native Americans. The Iroquois were on the attack throughout the east and even managed to extend their raids into the middle Ohio River Valley and the Illinois River Valley. These Iroquois onslaughts rendered Berrien County largely unsafe. Most of the tribal groups fled westward around Lake Michigan.

The Potawatomi were contacted first by Jean Nicolet, a Frenchman, in 1634. This event occurred considerably outside Berrien County. Using their own orthography, the French pronounced words originally derived from the Ottawa nation. Hence, the people whom Nicolet met he referred to as the Pouteouatami or the Oupouteouatamik. The Potawatomi called themselves Neshnabek (True Humans).

By 1653, the Potawatomi had become the dominant Native American tribe in the Green Bay area and had begun expanding back southward by a process of fissioning of their clans who then rapidly colonized new territories. By the late 1660s, the Potawatomi's control of the western shore of Lake Michigan gave them a major advantage in the fur trade which linked the Sioux country to the west with the French. French traders, whom the Great Lakes Native Americans originally saw simply as members of another tribal group, eventually began to arrive in greater numbers, and the Potwatomi representatives began undertaking the long trek to Montreal to meet with government officials. As the threat of the Iroquois attacks waned, other Native Americans slowly began to reoccupy the St. Joseph Valley.

The Potawatomi probably reached (returned to) the St. Joseph River in the late 1680s where they found the Miami already well established. By about 1706 they took control of the valley, with many of the Miami subsequently withdrawing slowly southward. This was not always a peaceful process. In 1711, a combined force of Potawatomi and Ottawa, led by Makisabe and Sagunia, destroyed a neighboring Mascouten village on the St. Joseph River. At least 150 people died in the attack. This further acerbated a long-standing enmity between the Fox (allies of the Mascouten and the British) and many of the Native Americans who were aligned with the French. Thus, by the Fox (Black Hawk) War of 1832, more than a century of traditional hostility existed involving the Fox tribe and other Native American groups and British-Americans.

In 1736 the Golden Carp, Frog, Crab, and Tortoise clans of the Potawatomi Water Phatry were all present along the river, and around 100 warriors could be mustered. They had forged a strong trade and military alliance between themselves and the French against the Iroquois and British, a friendship that would last until the late eighteenth century when French power in the Great Lakes disappeared. Many of the Potawatomi, including important tribal leaders such as Piremon and Wilamek, converted—at least nominally—to Catholicism. Wilamek served as LaSalle's guide to the St. Joseph River in 1679.

Along the river, the French built a fort and a mission. Named Fort St. Joseph, it was one of several such outposts, including those at Green Bay and Michilimackinac, constructed by the French to control the fur trade along the interconnecting waterways of the interior Great Lakes. Here, Native Americans would trade with the small resident French population, have some of their newly created spiritual needs administered to by the French black robes, serve as warriors with the French against their mutual enemies, and generally interact harmoniously with the white French interlopers until the 1760s. Many French traders took Native American wives and became members of their extended families. The children of these unions were later called *metis* and, upon French withdrawal, were looked down upon as half-breeds by both the British and, later, the Americans.

The barest of suggestions—likely a myth—is made that a small French mission was constructed near Indian Fields sometime during the eighteenth century. Lucius Lyon's survey map from 1830 noted during his platting of Oronoko Township that "Opposite the west bank is the old French Mission; we can see the antiquated crosses designating one of those places appointed for all living—when they came, what they did, and whither they are gone God only knows." No mention of this mission and its residents and activities has yet been discovered in any of the French documents covering the period, so it remains a mystery.

This location, however, would have been logical for a small Catholic mission. It was near this place along the St. Joseph River in 1721 that Charlevoix was almost shot and killed by a Native American who mistook him for a bear in the evening twilight. A Potawatomi village may have been in Indian Fields by this time (Big Wolf would settle here eventually). Two Indian trails met where the town now stands, and both roads are clearly depicted on the earliest government survey maps. Mr. Cunningham, who once had an interview with Lewis E. Kephart, said Kephart reported that in 1894 sixteen skeletons—some of them perhaps Native Americans—were unearthed at the south end of Main Street. A crew of workers who were mining gravel discovered the skeletons on the bluff overlooking the river. Pottery and prayer beads, which indicate an historic period date, were included with the burials. Nothing visible of the mission or the cemetery remains today.

Sometimes, I cannot help but wonder if knowing anything about the presence of Native Americans and the French mission in my hometown would have spurred me at an earlier age to consider archeology as a career. I lived a scant three blocks from the most possible site of the French mission and spent hundreds of hours at play in Indian Fields (the Grove). We roamed atop the river bluffs and hunted pheasants and rabbits in the fields where Native Americans had likewise sought game for their cooking pots.

One particular trek during a fall afternoon stands out vividly in my mind. It was mid-October in 1956 after school, and Bob Sherwood and I left his house on U.S. 31 and began wandering back toward the river. We grabbed some Red Delicious apples off a tree in a neighbor's orchard and skirted the fence surrounding the Kimmel farm where the flint blade cache and the Native American burial would soon be discovered. We continued into the woods along the high bluff and headed downriver across the Eidson and Wymer properties where Dr. Garland would excavate the remains of major Native American occupations. We kicked up some pheasants, but did not have our shotguns with us, so we sighted them with our fingers and fired. We apparently missed each one, and they quickly and noisily disappeared. Shortly before it became too dark for us to see our way clearly, we circled back through the campus of Emmanuel Missionary College (Andrews University since 1960) toward home. On that leisurely ramble we had walked across more than 3000 years of Berrien Springs' past, and no one was there to relate it to us.

The Dialect of the Tribe

On March 30, 1825, Indian Agent Alexander Wolcott sent a letter from his cramped headquarters at the small and rather insignificant frontier outpost named Chicago to his superior, Superintendent of Indian Affairs Lewis Cass. In this official report, Wolcott listed the various Native American villages under his wide geographical jurisdiction. Included in Wolcott's territory were eight permanent settlements along the St. Joseph River containing a total resident population of 843 individuals. Although tribalized in this document as Potawatomis, each of the villages undoubtedly contained Native Americans from a variety of different ethnic affiliations. An additional 16 members of the Ottawa nation resided in a village located somewhere along the "River Galene" (Galien).

Only a scant three years later, E. Reed, a Michigan Territorial officer (see page 24), was specifically assigned by Michigan Territorial Governor Cass to study the current situation concerning Native Americans along the St. Joseph River. Reed noted that the overall population of "Potawatomis" had dropped to a mere 175 people. In addition, the Ottawas' Galien River settlement appears to have disappeared altogether.

In the intervening three years, a number of significant events had gravely affected the St. Joseph River Potawatomi. First, with the expulsion of the Jesuits from North America in 1762, the Potawatomi no longer had direct access to the Catholic guardians of the faith. Into the breach had stepped Protestant missionaries from numerous denominations; a Baptist stronghold, the Carey Mission under the direction of Reverend Isaac McCoy, had been established near Niles in 1822. McCoy apparently held a favorable connection with some of the most important territorial and federal government officials, including Governor Cass. McCoy was ardently in favor of a mandated federal removal policy which would force all Native Americans to relocate themselves on reservations west of the Mississippi River. By 1825, Reverend McCoy was lobbying heavily and was directing his efforts specifically against the St. Joseph River Potawatomi. His labors bore the fruits he desired within a few years when the Indian Removal Act of 1830 was signed into federal law by President Andrew Jackson.

Second, since the late eighteenth century, the Potawatomi had been maneuvered into signing a series of disastrous treaties. Those of 1821 and 1828 resulted in the cession of nearly all of their remaining tribal estate in Michigan and northern Indiana to the United States. Ironically, the treaty of 1828 was held at the Carey Mission while Reverend McCoy—who had quietly removed himself from the scene—was in Kansas scouting for a suitable block of land for the proposed new Potawatomi reservation. From this 1828 treaty, only a few parcels of land were deeded back to the Potawatomi. Neither Indian Fields nor Big Wolf's village were among them.

Among the properties retained by the Potawatomi were Pokagon's village south of Niles and Moccasin's village north of Buchanan. The original Government Land Office plat map does not extend the section survey lines through the Moccasin's village property. A conspicuous blank spot is left on the map with a single notation that reads simply "Indian Territory," and both Moccasin's name and any reference to the Potawatomi are entirely omitted. After the village land was ceded to the government as an article in the Chicago Treaty of 1833, the survey lines were incorporated and the Territory was ready for sale to one or more homesteaders.

Reverend McCoy is a rather curious study. Historians and his biographers have characteristically pictured him as a pious, God-fearing, and generally charitable man. Interestingly enough, however, some of his contemporary white neighbors of the St. Joseph River Valley do not seem to have agreed. Timothy S. Smith in 1833 published a pamphlet entitled *Missionary Abominations Unmasked or A View of Carey Mission Containing an Unmasking of the Missionary Abominations Practiced Among the Indians of St. Joseph County at the Celebrated Missionary Establishment Known as CAREY MISSION under the Superintendence of the REV. ISAAC McCOY*. Smith, who had migrated to Berrien County from New England in 1826, charged that McCoy, among other alleged crimes, had diverted some of the funds donated to the mission for the "improvement" of the Potawatomi nation and the mission's farm land, equipment, and buildings directly into his own pocket. Thus, the Native American children under McCoy's guidance and pastoral care at the mission school, according to Smith, frequently had to go without adequate food, shelter, and clothing.

Without being willing to be completely explicit, Smith also hinted that McCoy was involved in selling whiskey to his charges. Further, Smith insinuated that Reverend McCoy had instigated a party of Potawatomi into harassing Squire Isaac Thompson, an early settler of Niles, who was supposedly in the same business. Presumably, in McCoy's eyes, Thompson was unwanted competition.

In a later volume published in 1899, *The Removal of the Pottawatomie (sic) Indians from Northern Indiana*, Daniel McDonald of Plymouth, Indiana, pointed out that McCoy's wife, Christiana (nee Polke), was the sister of a local judge, William Polke. Polke was a wealthy, influential, and early citizen of the Plymouth area of northern Indiana. While still a youth living at Kincheloe's Station in Nelson County, Kentucky, the future judge had been kidnapped by the Potawatomi and brought north to one of their villages along the St. Joseph River. After more than three years in captivity, he was finally returned to his family in Kentucky. He then migrated back to the territory of northern Indiana where he settled permanently. A few years later, in 1832, Judge Polke erected the first frame house built north of the Wabash River.

Polke assisted his brother-in-law, Reverend McCoy, for a time at the Carey Mission. Apparently, they worked hand in hand in order to see that all of the remaining Native American claims to their land in southern Michigan and northern Indiana were extinguished and orders were given for the Native Americans' immediate removal westward. Thus, Judge Polke not only extracted revenge for his kidnapping many years earlier, but he also managed to purchase an enormous tract of former Potawatomi land in extreme northern Indiana. He was subsequently appointed to the powerful position of Government Removal Agent, so he personally oversaw some of the Potawatomis' final dispossession of their former tribal estate.

McDonald accumulated and published a number of eye-witness accounts about the removal of the Potawatomi from both Native Americans and from whites employed to see that the Potawatomi expeditiously abandoned their ancestral homes. The Potawatomi were permitted one last visit to their tribal cemeteries to weep for the last time, "never to look upon the graves of their kindred again." And "nearly one thousand men, women, and children with broken hearts and tearful eyes, took up the march to their far western home." Their villages were torn down by the soldiers and "had the appearance of having been swept by a hurricane." One hundred and fifty Native Americans died while on this forced march to the Kansas territory.

Finally, McCoy labored mightily to see Catholicism eradicated from the tribes. Father Benjamin Marie Petit spoke about the removal in 1838: "I shall have to level the altar and the church to the ground, and bury the cross which overshadows the tombs to save them from profanation." This "profanation" to which Father Petit refers was contamination from Protestantism. Here, however, Reverend McCoy's efforts would be doomed to partial failure as many of the Potawatomis remained firmly embedded within the Catholic faith. Some of them have remained so until the present time.

McCoy's religious proselytizing had only a minimal impact on many of the Potawatomi people. Indeed, by 1830, a delegation of Potawatomi led by Leopold Pokagon (who died ca. 1841) had journeyed to Detroit to request a priest from Father Gabriel Richard. The elder Pokagon's speech to Father Richard began as follows: "Father, Father, I come again to beseech you to give us a Black Robe who will make known the word of God." Pokagon also obliquely referred to McCoy in his petition: "There is an American minister who wishes to bring us to his religion; but neither I nor any of my village have been willing to send our children to his school, or to assist at his sermons; we have kept our custom of praying, as the Black Robe formerly at [Fort] St. Joseph's instructed our fathers."

Father Richard responded positively by dispatching Father Stephen Badin westward to the frontier to minister to the Potawatomi. Not only "Indians" but also further identified as Catholics (Badin had baptized more than six hundred Potawatomi by 1833), these people stood apart from their white and largely Protestant neighbors. In their subsequent, and generally heated, negotiations with government officials over the next several years, these particular Potawatomi were frequently referred to as "the Catholic party."

The local Potawatomi had few defenders during the turbulent nineteenth century other than their Catholic priests. Hoping to dispel some of the erroneous ideas that outsiders had of Native

Americans, Father Louis Baroux—who was assigned to the St. Joseph River country—wrote to his superior from the Sacred Heart of Mary Catholic Church of Silver Creek in 1862. He said that the Native Americans were not *"MAN EATERS"* (his capitals); and further, "They say in France that in 100 years this race of people will entirely disappear. That is not my way of thinking. The teachings of the Gospel will give them a new viewpoint and perspective and introduce them to civilization." Baroux remained hopeful for their future even though he was somewhat patronizing in his tone.

These stories swirling around the head of Reverend McCoy and the Potawatomis would have constituted excellent morality tales for our American History class. In 1956, the civil-rights movement was just underway with the explosive events taking place in Alabama. Another dispossessed ethnic group was actively seeking public recognition and a well-earned redress. An historical example of a duplicity this large—and a scandalous one at that—residing squarely in our own backyard would certainly have enlivened an otherwise dull class, bringing close to home a process that already had a long-standing tradition in American society. In retrospect, I suppose this would have been extremely dangerous knowledge for our young minds.

By the late 1830s, many of the Potawatomis were in full retreat with heavily laden caravans carrying whole families to Kansas on the aptly named "Trail of Death." Some of the St. Joseph River Potawatomi eventually settled with Father Hoecken, S.J., on Potawatomi Creek in Kansas while others remained with McCoy. One band, however, chose to remain in Michigan. They exercised a codicil in the Chicago Treaty of 1833 that was poorly understood by the whites. Those who remained would come down to us today as the Catholic Potawatomi, or, more specifically in southwestern Michigan, as Pokagon's Band.

This codicil embodied a key American cultural value: the governed must first consent to any government action that directly affects them. Those Potawatomi aligned under the leadership of Leopold Pokagon emphatically did not consent to being removed to far-off, mysterious Kansas (Indian Territory). After much argument and negotiation stretching across several years, these Catholic Potawatomi were allowed to remain in southwestern Michigan.

Under Leopold Pokagon's leadership, the Potawatomi sold their remaining Berrien County land and used the proceeds to purchase 847 acres around Silver Creek in Cass County in 1837. At this date, the total white population of Berrien County was 4,863; Blois's *Gazetteer* estimates that about 100 Native Americans were left. The Pokagons later bought several additional parcels in Van Buren County. Thus, they began to adapt to the new political conditions imposed upon them by following, first of all, the traditional American procedure of buying land privately. This constituted a major cultural change for them. Previously, land could not be owned by a single individual but was held in trust by an entire clan. Access to the land in the past had been strictly guaranteed to all kinship members in good standing. Successful cultural adaptation required both the acquiring of new values and a restructuring of old ones.

Further, when United States Secretary of War Hugh Brady ordered the removal of Native Americans from Michigan in 1840, by force if necessary, his enforcing army was met by an armed party of civilians, accompanied by a few soldiers, with a writ from Michigan Supreme Court Judge Epaphroditus Ransom. (Ransom had recently tried the first case to be held in the new Berrien County courthouse in Berrien Springs on April 11, 1839.) The writ stated outright that the Potawatomi had a legal right to continue to live on their own land if they elected to do so. They did and have been resident in southwestern Michigan ever since. Thus, the Potawatomi had come to understand and to exploit for their own benefit the new political system that had been imposed upon them.

Still, much prejudice remained. Even fifty years later, this prejudicial mid-nineteenth-century attitude toward Native Americans can be clearly seen in a slender volume entitled *Six Months Among the Indians* by Darius B. Cook. (Originally published in 1889, it was reissued in 1983.) Cook, for many years, was the editor of the *Niles Mirror*. Hence, he was an individual of considerable influence in shaping the perspectives and attitudes of his local readership toward not only the Potawatomi but also toward all Native Americans.

In 1840, as a young man in poor health, Cook and a male companion left Berrien County and undertook a trip to the wilds of Allegan County which at that time had virtually no white resident population. They lived in a small cabin near the present town of Wayland with only a single white family in their immediate neighborhood. A significant number of Native Americans, including some important tribal figures such as Saginaw, Noonday, and Gosa, had established encampments nearby.

The boys subsisted largely off the land, hunting deer and trapping wolves. The book is replete with tall tales involving vicious attacks by man-eating wolves which certainly served to reinforce negative opinions concerning these important predators. Prejudices against Native Americans, who are referred to in the book as "savages," are also scattered throughout the narrative written some fifty years after his sojourn. He concludes the volume by admitting that the "friendless Indian" has been shorn of a birthright, land, homes, and graves of ancestors. But he states this opinion: "An inferior race must yield to a superior, who will have no respect for their rights. Another century will wipe out every vestige of the Indian race on the American continent and they will be only known in history." Cook, of course, was premature in his judgment.

Cook's own intellectual perspective of Native Americans had been formed during the mid-nineteenth century. Cook was a true child of the Enlightenment, a period when all of the so-called primitives of the world were classified by European and American scholars as merely ignorant people caught in the trap of false thinking. These scholars viewed Native Americans, for example, as being unable to grasp the idea that unseen causes could have far-reaching effects. Since they lacked a germ theory of disease, Native Americans attributed some illnesses and other infectious disasters to witches and/or other malevolent beings. They responded to disease accordingly with herbs administered by shamans, dances, or incantations that European and American observers rejected as patently false. Intellectually, in the eyes of most white people, the Native Americans were doomed not only to cultural failure but to eventual biological extinction. Social Darwinism had encountered fertile soil in which to grow and flourish in the wilds of the New World.

This same denigrating attitude pervades most early local histories. David Schwartz, who penned the section on Oronoko Township in Ellis' *History of Berrien and Van Buren Counties* (1880), appears to have interviewed the widow of Hezekiah Hall who had homesteaded near Berrien Springs in 1832. Hall's widow recalled her early life on a lonely farm in the wilderness of southwestern Michigan. Schwartz writes concerning "her first terror at the appearance of Indians…[when her husband was away in Niles] her terrors were increased by the appearance at her cabin of Indians, but she kept up a brave heart, nevertheless, although as it happened the *savages* were harmless enough. She often saw them in *grand carousals* and *fantastic dances* on the river-bluff, opposite her cabin" (my emphasis).

Schwartz continues in a similar vein with a second widow, Mrs. Michael Hand, who along with her husband and his nephew had homesteaded in section 30 of Berrien Township in 1831. He paraphrases her as saying, "between the howling of wolves, apprehensions touching the near presence of *savages,* and the consciousness that they were far from neighbors, life was far from pleasant" (my emphasis). Both the wolves and Native Americans take their shots from Schwartz, and the Native Americans' status as honorable human beings is constantly being called into question.

Since 1840, the Potawatomi have been consistently embroiled in various legal battles over their dual status as Native Americans and citizens as well as over the repatriations that are due them from the several treaties they were often tricked into signing. They have met with only limited success in these endeavors. They did not begin to collect the annuities awarded to them until finally in 1866, some 30 years after they were to have been paid. Thus, even before the middle of the nineteenth century, they had lost the bulk of their ancient landholdings and had had their annual pattern of movements vastly curtailed by white settlement. Added to these factors was the intense prejudice they encountered on an almost daily basis. Even well into the 1960s, according to Evertt Claspy in his *The Potawatomi Indians of Southwestern Michigan* (1966), they were still refused service in some restaurants in the town of Hartford.

Still, despite three centuries of intense outside pressures, the Native Americans have maintained their own identity as a separate social unit through adhering to, as James Clifton phrases it in his monograph *The Pokagons, 1683-1983*, "their status as Indians; their distinctive band heritage; the band's political organization; community, family, and kin; and the Catholic Church." Because they have endured and because their ancestors have been so long resident in southwestern Michigan, they cannot be ignored as an integral part of the region's past.

A Strong Brown God

*A*s far back as I can remember, I have never been tremendously enamored with eating fish. This culinary ambivalence—certainly a technical avoidance rather than a formal cultural taboo—extends to both the fresh and salt water varieties. Yet, the act of fishing was an entirely different phenomenon. Particularly during my younger days, fishing was a pursuit I always found worth engaging in. However, this intensely intellectual endeavor could be met only under one of two sets of very specific types of fishing. The St. Joseph River met both of them admirably.

The first of these was the ancient art of dip-netting. My buddies and I pursued this activity during the spring sucker run as the fish laboriously made their way up the river from Lake Michigan to spawn. It was conducted from wooden plank piers that jutted well out into the river below the dam that impounds Lake Chapin, the point at which the migrating red horse suckers were turned back by the massive earth and concrete barrier. Large dip nets were attached to a pole and winch, allowing the nets to be cranked up and down at our leisure. Smaller, hand-held nets were employed to remove the wriggling catch which sometimes included carp or an occasional eel. The captured fish were dumped unceremoniously into burlap gunny sacks tied tightly to the pier by a rope. As a final step, these bags could be lowered back into the water to keep each day's catch alive and fresh.

Dip-netting was a most leisurely pursuit, one especially enticing to teenage boys. Each dip-net rig had a small enclosed shelter constructed directly on the pier. Here, we could lounge, away from the cold and bitter spring winds, and smoke forbidden cigarettes, read, or engage in idle conversation about the most pressing international subjects of the day—girls and how to ask them

The dam and Lake Chapin around 1915.

for dates, cars (of course), our minimal allowances, our overburdening chores, the never-ending homework, or baseball. Every 15 minutes or so, one of us would arise and wheel up the net to check for a catch, hoping for a 25-pound carp or a mess of suckers. All thoughts of any after-school chores or our homework were completely lost in the dying afternoon light.

Carp and suckers were never eaten (by any of us at least, since we considered them garbage fish); instead, they were sold immediately to a man I remember only as Heine. Heine had his place of business on U. S. 31 directly across the bridge from town. There he maintained a number of large fish ponds where suckers and carp could be kept alive until their eventual purchase. We sold our day's catch to him for around five cents a pound which he, in turn, resold for ten cents a pound or more. In a spring afternoon during the spawning run, following—in our opinion—the overly long school day, we could each earn two dollars or more for scarcely any real output of heavy, intensive labor.

The second type of fishing was an even more relaxing venture, again one demanding the most minimal physical exertion. A casting rod and reel, night crawlers picked up in the yard at dusk for bait, and a Y-shaped stick were all we required. We would cast out the line baited with a night crawler and equipped with a heavy sinker, drive the stick into the ground, and place the rod into the Y. Then, book in hand, we'd sit back comfortably on the river bank for the remainder of the day. If luck held steady and true, we were able to go home without ever noticing whether or not we had had even a single bite.

The St. Joseph River had been a crucial lifeline to Native Americans ever since their initial entry into southwestern Michigan thousands of years ago. *Shag-wah-se-be*, or Mystery River, was a Potawatomi name which roughly translates as a reference to the (seemingly) spontaneous fungal (or mushroom and toadstool) growths occurring widely along its banks. In typical European fashion, the river was immediately renamed during the late seventeenth century by the French priests who called it "River of the Miamis" after the Native Americans they initially found living along its shores in Berrien County. Eventually, a few decades later in the eighteenth century, the French clergy changed the name again to "St. Joseph."

To rename a landmark is, linguistically and symbolically, to take formal possession of and hence to culturally alter. With these dual results emanating from the aggressive act of reclassification, the effective control and use of the Shag-wah-se-be gradually passed from the original Native American inhabitants to the European interlopers and, ultimately, to the American homesteaders who arrived in all-out force beginning in the early nineteenth century.

The headwaters for the river lie to the east in Baw Beese Lake in Hillsdale County. The river's course of approximately 200 miles, during which it drains about 4,300 square miles, takes its first southwestwardly turn into northeastern Indiana and then meanders slowly westward until a sharp turn carries the stream back north and through Berrien County to its outlet into Lake Michigan. During its cross-country voyage, the river drops nearly 521 feet in elevation.

The Shag-wah-se-be was once a remarkably placid stream containing only three kickpoints. These abrupt changes in gradient existed before several dams were thrown up in the early twentieth century. Prior to this human interference, no significant waterfalls or major rapids hindered either spawning fish or birchbark-canoe travel along the river's entire length. This easily navigable river was greatly appreciated both by the Native Americans, in particular the local groups such as Potawatomis who were widely acknowledged as master canoeists, and later by French fur traders, the voyageurs.

The first of these kickpoints is located in Berrien Springs just below Lake Chapin dam which spans the river some twenty miles from its mouth at the city of St. Joseph. The St. Joseph River in this first section of its valley is gentle with an average gradient of one foot per mile as it cuts through two late glacial moraines, termed the Lake Border and Valparaiso. The valley is about one mile across and is bordered by steep bluffs. It contains a well-developed meander pattern with meander cut-offs and a well-drained flood plain, all of which indicates system maturity to the geologist. More obvious youthful features include point bars (denoting active deposition) and steep, heavily timbered bluffs. It was this part of the river, from its first kickpoint up to the head of Lake Chapin, that I knew best.

The earliest American settlers, following the Native American and French example, quickly recognized the river's vast potential for transporting cargo. In 1829, well before many of the present towns including Berrien Springs had even been platted and while Michigan was still a territory with statehood a mere dream, Congress authorized a survey of the river to determine the practicality of connecting it by canal with the Wabash River well to the southwest. Howard Stansbury, who had surveyed some of Berrien County's lands with Lucius Lyon, estimated that a canal from the town of St. Joseph to South Bend, alone, would cost $480,000. Congress balked at this enormous sum, and in the end no federal funds were ever appropriated for this herculean task.

But that in no way deterred commercial use of the river. Steamboats were already plying the river by 1833 with the *Matilda Barney* making regular trips between Niles and St. Joseph. By the early 1830s, keelboats, and in 1834 a second steamboat—the *Davy Crockett* (whose namesake would fall at the Alamo two years later), joined the growing flotilla. Shortly thereafter, two additional steamers, the *Patronage* and the *Pocahontas,* were also seen navigating the river. Grain, lumber, wool, flour, fresh fruit, and whiskey flowed regularly downstream where they were exchanged for dry goods and hardware supplies in St. Joseph.

The budding town of St. Joseph had become a major, if local, port, and the trade and intervillage communications provided by the river were indispensable for the small communities beginning to emerge and mature along its shores. In 1838, State of Michigan hydrologists determined that $93,868 would be required to complete a series of necessary channel improvements, like the removal of impediments such as fallen trees and boulders, between St. Joseph and the Indiana state line (a distance of 48.5 river miles). This dredging work was to insure a constant depth of five feet of water. Somehow the money was raised for this particular endeavor and much of the river was subsequently improved for steamboat navigation.

Until 1851, traffic on the river was regular and constant. In 1840, for example, 41,758 barrels of flour and 1,700 casks of whiskey reached port in St. Joseph from the interior. In 1844, these figures grew to 129,333 barrels of flour and 2,721 casks of whiskey. Coffee, tea, and white sugar were among the goods now required by the new settlements upriver. By this time, around 60 keelboats were navigating the St. Joseph River in addition to the many steamers and uncounted canoes. However, in 1850, the newly approved Michigan State Constitution mandated that all funds for the improvement of internal transportation facilities were to be allocated solely for public wagon roads. Henceforth, no new monies would be allotted for maintaining any of the waterways, including locally essential ones such as the St. Joseph River.

So ended the mighty influence of the St. Joseph River, the strong brown god. By the middle of the nineteenth century, another mode of transportation was deemed more essential than water travel. Railroads began to make their presence felt. In 1851, the *Southern Road* arrived at South Bend, and river traffic was vastly curtailed. By 1852, significant inland riverine shipping was at an end forever in southwestern Michigan.

Berrien Springs never had a formal, electric streetcar line though the interurban—the Southern Michigan Railway—did travel through the town from 1906 until the company's bankruptcy in 1934. Crossing the river from the south on the longest interurban bridge in the world, it passed down Main Street, the widest avenue in town, directly in front of my great grandparents' boarding house. (One of the conductors in 1906 was my great grandfather, John C. Hoopingarner.) In *Michigan History Magazine* (Nov./Dec., 1993), an old photograph shows the train just as it is beginning to enter the bridge in order to transverse the river from Main Street. This picture dates prior to the construction of the dam, and Lake Chapin did not yet exist. The river appears to be extremely narrow and swampy at this point. The abandoned piles of the interurban still stand out starkly in Lake Chapin today.

A narrow gauge railway line, the St. Joseph Valley Railroad, was constructed between Buchanan and Berrien Springs in 1880,

PUBLISHED BY THE NOVELTY SUPPLY CO., NILES, MICH.
FOR W. F. ... LEY, BERRIEN SPRINGS, MICH.

THE
LONGEST INTERURBAN R. R. BRIDGE
IN THE WORLD,
BERRIEN SPRINGS, MICH.

A train on what was the longest interurban bridge
in the world—probably from the early 1900s.

but it went into receivership in 1886. One of its directors was George Murdoch of Berrien Springs. Another important backer of this particular railroad was Fred McOmber, editor of several successive newspapers including the Berrien Springs *Era*. In 1889, Jonas Burns from Goshen, Indiana, purchased the company, converted the tracks to standard gauge, and graded the roadbed. Then Burns, too, went broke. A group of Chicago business people made an additional valiant attempt to cross the county with tracks; they also failed by 1893. Although the St. Joseph Valley Railway closed in 1893, it reopened as the Milwaukee, Benton Harbor and Columbus Railway in 1897 and was extended to Benton Harbor. The Pere Marquette Railroad bought it in 1903 and operated the line until 1922.

The absence of a functional railroad, coupled with the loss of river traffic, was one of the major factors that prompted the transfer of the county seat from Berrien Springs to the larger metropolis of St. Joseph in 1894. Rapid transportation and improved communication were now not only a dream—they had become American necessities; and these modern conveniences were totally lacking in Berrien Springs. The placid, meandering river could not compete unaided. And a functioning railroad undoubtedly would have been a mixed blessing.

Turner commented in 1867 that Berrien Springs "is innocent

of railroads, which accounts for the fact that, although very pleasantly located and enjoying many great natural advantages, it has
only about 1,000 people. This cannot remain so long." Happily, for
my own boyhood, this innocence—despite that minor blip in the
late nineteenth and early twentieth centuries—did remain so for
long. And it still does today.

Any ultimate hopes, however faint, that one may have had for
a return to a regular and continuous river transportation system
were finally dashed with the damming of the river. A total of nine
containment structures were eventually built. The Indiana and
Michigan Electric Company (I & M) constructed their concrete
dam at Berrien Springs in 1908, assuring constant and much
appreciated hydroelectric power for the village. The lake that rapidly formed upriver behind the impoundment was formally chris-
tened Lake Chapin in honor of Charles Chapin, son of Henry
Austin Chapin of Niles, one of the county's wealthier (partly from
Upper Peninsula iron-ore investments, among other things) citizens. Among the elder Chapin's numerous business ventures was
a significant financial interest in I & M. The younger Chapin was
president of I & M and a principal promoter of the endeavor.

I have a postcard taped to my office wall. One side has a color
aerial photograph of the dam and Lake Chapin. It was sent to me
by a former graduate student of mine from eastern Indiana who
had, at one time, been married to a Buchanan girl. The photograph
is undated, but was probably taken in the 1980s. The caption refers
to the reservoir as the "lovely Lake Chapin." However, as I recall,
in 1956 Lake Chapin was viewed by most of my teenage peers and
me as a rather useless body of dirty, fetid, and smelly water.

No one fished there in the 1950s, and I don't recall ever seeing
any kind of pleasure craft on the waters of the lake at any time.
Lake Chapin was generally avoided by everyone. Several of us
boys once discovered, in a field outside of town, a badly beaten-
up sailboat which we repaired to the best of our ability. We somehow acquired a functional sail and spent that summer sailing on
the waters of Indian Lake and Lake Michigan. Even though Lake
Chapin was right at hand, we never even considered launching
our make-shift craft there. In fact, I do not remember it ever having been a subject for discussion. Perhaps we feared that we might
suddenly be caught in the wind and plunge headlong over the
dam. It was apparently assumed by all of us that Lake Chapin
simply was not adequate for our recreational boating purposes.

I do remember swimming in the lake a few times above the dam, at the Grove near the interurban abutments. I was expressly forbidden to do so by my mother, but secretly persevered anyway. The last time I ever entered the water there, I jumped from the badly rotting pier feet first. When I resurfaced, I knew immediately that something was wrong. I had cut my right foot rather severely on a submerged broken bottle and had to limp home several long and agonizing blocks, trailing copious amounts of blood. I still have the jagged scar as a reminder of Lake Chapin.

I believe that the river and the lake fascinated some of my friends as well. As kids, often in groups, we played along the bluffs and banks of the river on an almost daily basis. We built forts and hideaways and cached our treasures, using this body of water as a backdrop for dreaming about the present. The swirling, silt-laden water was a moving presence just over the hillside and down the slope. When it beckoned, I always responded willingly.

Late one afternoon, Hunter Watson, "Stork" Schauber, and I decided to go fishing overnight on an island in the river. After setting up camp, we began gathering firewood. Long into the night we made plans for fishing trips to come. One of these—a several-days' venture by canoe down northern Michigan's Black River—actually came to fruition. When the fire had burned low and the wood was almost exhausted, Stork climbed a tree and began dancing on a dead limb to bring it down. He was successful, but descended in a crashing heap with it. Hunter's and my diagnosis, amid Stork's mournful cries, was that it would be some time before he was once again capable of breeding.

By 1956, the river and its past apparently played little if any significant role in the active memory of the town's adults. They had forgotten, for instance, that at one time the back swamps had been the source of Michigan ague, a form of malarial fever that had severely plagued the earliest homesteaders in the county. This ague caused several deaths. The ailment was arrested in the mid-nineteenth century after quinine was found to be a successful cure. These fetid swamps and marshes along the river were never forbidden territory to us, and we searched intensely for snakes and snapping turtles in these same wet morasses a century later. Since we were unable to identify most of these snakes, they all became—in our young minds—deadly poisonous and greatly dreaded cottonmouth water moccasins.

One has to read far back in time to find descriptions from an era when the river functioned in any essential role for the village. One of Turner's anonymous sources commented in the 1860s that Berrien Springs overlooked "the beautiful St. Joseph" which "is a thing of beauty, bordered and embowered with the sycamore, black walnut, buckeye, papaw and wild grape; and as a place for rambles, walks and drives, is unsurpassed for romantic loveliness and sylvan beauty." Even in the early twentieth century, the Grove was considered, at least by the *Journal Era* (April 6, 1916), potentially the finest resort facility in southern Michigan. It even boasted a pleasure boat, the *Laura May*, for tourist excursions. By the 1950s, the resort business was largely extinct due to the heavy amounts of sewage that had been dumped into the river upstream. None of my elders ever related stories to me about any past river or lake adventures, and I never knew of any adults who would admit to having ever rambled along their banks or who considered them things of beauty.

The U.S. 31 bridge generally seemed in good repair (except in 1948 when it suddenly dropped into the river), so we never had any traffic delays in crossing it to drive south to Niles or east to Eau Claire. The village is set high on the bluff far above the active flood plain where no houses were located. Only when a massive flood inundated U.S. 31 across the bridge to the east of the river was any concern expressed. On some occasions during the spring, runoff from melting snow caused the road to be submerged under several feet of brown, muddy water. But it was apparently only a

The *Laura May* around 1915.

minor bother. One could still drive to Niles via Buchanan or to Eau Claire through Benton Harbor, and our daily lives could continue without interruption.

Yet, how severe were these floods of my memory? In the 1970s, the Federal Insurance Administration of the Department of Housing and Urban Development authorized a flood control survey of the St. Joseph River. Among the several townships abutting the river, neither Oronoko nor Berrien had public reports filed on them. Those that did submit reports include Niles, St. Joseph, Benton, Royalton, and Sodus, along with several townships that suffered heavy beach erosion along Lake Michigan. In retrospect, I suspect that the floods of the 1950s and my boyhood were more of an annoyance to the town folks than a disaster. And, certainly, being overlooked by the federal government can't be all that bad.

Early one spring in the mid 1950s, Lake Chapin was drained to allow for some repairs on the dam. I walked along the old river channel on the slowly drying, cracking mud flats. I came across the skeleton of an extremely large fish. Today, knowing that lake sturgeon was the dominant fish exploited by local Native Americans and was once one of the more abundant species in the river, I like to believe that that is what was lying there before me. Still, even had it been identified to me as a lake sturgeon, that fact would obviously have meant little to me then. Like my fellow residents, the river's past unfortunately was not an active part of my memory either.

In my high-school yearbook, the *Canoe* (an appropriate name for a volume of memorabilia from a small town along the St. Joseph River), there is a picture of me and four of my friends—Bob Sherwood, Linda Jones, Sandy Balough, and Yvonne Forbes. We are holding an old wagon wheel that we discovered during the drawdown while exploring along that long-since-drowned terrace. Nearby was the skeleton of a horse. The horse and wheel inspired far more interest in me than did those bleached fish bones. No, I am intellectually (if not emotionally) convinced that the fish I by-passed so disdainfully that late autumn afternoon was not the skeletal memory of an ancient lake sturgeon. More likely, it was merely a big, and recent, interloper: just an old carp that had been caught in an event over which it had no control or any understanding.

The Directory of Directors

*A*s a teenager in the 1950s, I never consciously thought at any great length about the surnames of my high-school peers. Even though a significant number of them worshipped at the local German Lutheran Church, and some of them were graduates of the German Lutheran parochial elementary school on Mechanic Street, a block from my great grandmother's house, I never really connected them directly to German ancestry. They were not truly German in the sense that, when I saw them, I imagined anything from that real Germany somewhere far off in Europe. In my mind, they had no necessary connection with World War II or with Hitler and the Nazis. I never heard any of them or their parents, or even their grandparents for that matter, speaking German. Plus, their names were quite easily pronounceable. I obviously exempted my own household in this regard, notwithstanding the fact that my mother's maiden name was Hoopingarner and that I lived in the Hoopingarner family home.

Hence, none of these classmates and close friends could have conceivably been born into family units that were foreign in origin. All of our families were 100 percent totally and purely "American." Our ancestors obviously had all resided right here since the beginning of recorded time, and probably even earlier than this obscure date, whenever that might have been. In essence, then, none of us had any imaginable past that projected our biological forebears or cultural background beyond the territorial limits of the United States and its discovery and founding, or, for most of us, even outside the familiar geography of Berrien County.

Over the last several decades, academicians in the social sciences have loved to debate the issues surrounding what ethnic influences might be responsible for the variability in underlying cultural ethos among the counties and subregions in the Middle West. A number of journal articles and books published by the 1940s had firmly drawn the battle lines: New Englanders in league with New Yorkers versus the Germans. They intensely debated one question: Which of these cultural heritages has had the greater impact upon local character developments?

Yet, as early as 1867, T. G. Turner in his *Gazetteer of the St. Joseph Valley, Michigan and Indiana* had chosen sides when he recorded the following passages concerning the excellent quality of life to be discovered in Berrien County, Michigan:

> A large proportion of the emigration into this, as into most of the other counties in Southern Michigan, has been from New England and New York. This fact accounts for the high degree of perfection to which the common schools have there been brought. The first public improvement a New England man looks to in a new country is a school house, and until this is completed he does not begin to feel at home. . . . For it his money, however laboriously earned, goes freely. He looks upon it with the pride of a prince, and when he sees his children marching, in cleanly attired [sic], to this rudimentary temple of learning, he glows. . . . It is not, therefore, strange that Berrien County rejoices in the superiority of her common schools. No better exist anywhere. . . . To this fact may be attributed the general intelligence of the people.

Turner's assertion is to the point and his position is clear. Berrien County residents' excellence was due to the stock of its settlers— white and British with generational roots deep in American soil.

The 1893 *Portrait and Biographical Record of Berrien and Cass Counties, Michigan* presented short accounts of over 400 county residents currently living or just recently deceased. One hundred and seven of these were immigrants from New York State and 35 were from New England; another 22 were born in Berrien County of New York immigrants and four were offspring of New England immigrant parents. Thus, of the 407 for which I have data (and we are never informed of the specific method by which the honorees were chosen—though they certainly paid a fee for inclusion), 40.1 percent are of New York/New England heritage. In contrast, only 24 German immigrants, along with 10 of their children who were born in the county (an overall total of 34 or 8.2%), are so featured. New England/New York appears to be the obvious victor; and

Berrien County, as Turner had so forcefully averred in his description, could thus draw considerable home pride in situating itself squarely on this side of the heritage argument.

Reading elsewhere, however, I discovered, much to my surprise, that in the 1890 census (three years before this set of biographies was published) 3,491 individuals living in Berrien County had listed themselves as "foreign born, of German descent." In short, just fewer than one percent of the entire German population resident in the county was deemed worthy of inclusion among its social paragons. On the one hand, statistically, there appears to be a major sampling error present in the data. Native-born residents may have had more disposable income than immigrants with which to buy a biography. But on the other hand, the county may have been trying to set forth a certain image with the individuals featured. From yet another perspective, and less charitably I might add, we appear to have uncovered a late nineteenth-century ethnic bias, one which was actively striving to keep these native-born Germans and their first-generation descendants inexorably anchored to the lower end of Berrien County's status grading scale.

Although the data are incomplete for several of the following categories, we can use this volume of biographies to reconstruct the ideal citizen of Berrien County during the Gay Nineties. Our paragon was male. (Only two women have their own biographies as individuals—all other women are discussed only within the context of their husbands.) He was white (no Blacks or Native Americans need apply). He was also most likely Protestant. Some 89.3 percent list some form of Protestantism as their faith; of these, 51.4 percent are Methodist (the largest number at 26.8%), Congregationalist, or Baptist. There were no Jews.

Sixteen gentlemen list themselves as Catholic. Each of them is either foreign-born or is a first-generation offspring of foreign-born parents (eight German, six Irish, and one each from Canada and Poland). A considerable anti-Catholic sentiment was evident in the county. For example, Judge Thomas O'Hara of Niles (and later Berrien Springs) was defeated for reelection as Circuit Judge by Judge O. W. Coolidge in 1893 on what his biographer refers to as a heavy anti-Catholic vote.

Politically, our ideal citizen was assuredly a Republican (some 63.4% listed this political affiliation, as opposed to only 30.4% Democrats). Among the others, 18 individuals reported that they had switched to the Prohibition Party, and one was a Greenbacker.

Occupationally, around 60 percent gave their primary livelihood as deriving from farming, and 28.5 percent were in some form of business. There were 18 judges or lawyers, and 23 doctors, dentists, and veterinarians. The remainder were scattered among bankers, newspaper staff, Protestant ministers, teachers, and postmasters.

One hundred and ninety-seven of these Berrien County residents belonged to a lodge or social organization. Most popular were the Ancient and Free Accepted Masons and the Independent Order of Odd Fellows. Also important were the farm Granges and the G.A.R. (Grand Army of the Republic) for Civil War veterans. Two insurance companies, the Farmers Mutual Fire and Woodmen of the World, had local clubs. Mr. Daniel Williams Swen of Weesaw Township is noted as the president of the Anti-Horse Thief Association.

Even if most of their ancestors had not made the local-400 list, Berrien Springs and my own common school (a term that dates back to 1640 Massachusetts) were heavily populated with people of German biological and cultural background. These schools may have owed their ultimate existence to a New England/New York (Yankee) influence or, perhaps more properly, to the Land Ordinance of 1785 which required that one school be built in every new township. Families with surnames such as Ewalt, Kephart, Kesterke, Kimmel, Schinkel, Schinske, Schlutt, Schlutz, Schmall, Schmidt, Zech, and Zielke were scattered on farms throughout Oronoko Township. My own maternal great grandfather, John C. Hoopingarner, although he had originally migrated north from the town of Butler in Steuben County, Indiana, was of German background in his distant ancestral past.

One of the men responsible for the early growth of Berrien Springs was Dr. Philip Kephart (possibly originally Gebahard) who arrived in the new town in 1841 from Somerset County, Pennsylvania, and had been born in Tarryown, Maryland, in 1807. He married Susanna Kimmel, whose father came to Berrien Springs in 1829 and eventually homesteaded some 10,000 acres. (One of Daniel Boone's daughters, Martha, married Kimmel's son George in 1848.) Kephart was chosen by his pioneer peers to serve as the first village president. Part of the original Kephart estate was eventually purchased by Muhammad Ali for his permanent home.

German immigrants began their settlement of the Territory of Michigan during the 1820s. Ann Arbor, for example, was founded in 1828. In 1834, German traveler Karl Neidhard remarked in his

**Dr. Philip Kephart, elected as the
first village president.**

Reise Nach Michigan that "the little town of Ann Arbor looks fresh-ly carved and painted, as if it had stepped out of a Nurenberg toyshop only yesterday." At the time, Ann Arbor contained about sixty newly immigrated German families. When I arrived in Ann Arbor in the fall of 1958 to begin college, only two "ethnic" restau-rants operated in the city. Both were German and were extremely popular with the students, particularly for their German brands of draft beer. However, this ethnicity, unless one was part of the inner community, extended outward only to German cuisine.

Neidhard took considerable pains in his essay to explain, in his opinion, why the Germans were faring so well and expanding so rapidly in their new homeland. They were, he tells us, highly skilled, frugal, and able "to adapt themselves quickly to new con-ditions." They readily gave up their old cultural behaviors and daily habits when they deemed it necessary, willingly acquiring better techniques—such as more efficient farming methods—whenever they were presented. They had brought their old social environment along with them, including their German Lutheran form of Protestantism with its highly valued work ethic (drawn directly from one of Martin Luther's original theses). In the adap-tive process, they vastly increased their overall economic stand-ing. They contacted each other only for mutual aid, seldom spoke ill of one another, and were far more interested in "ax swinging" than in "fiddle playing." In short, they valued hard manual labor over leisure and were willing to endure extensive, long-term privation in order to lay the foundation for a better life in the future.

This stricture is clearly seen in the 1893 biographies volume. For instance, one Joseph U. Dohm, a Sodus Township farmer, included the following statement in his essay: "The paternal grandparents, born, reared, and married in the Fatherland [Germany], were in humble circumstances and trained up their children to habits of thrift and strict economy." Or, as my mother used to tell me ever so frequently, "Quit your bellyaching and get to work." I usually complied.

Thus, the basic underlying structure of the heritage of these Germans was well established long before the onset of their immigration into the United States and eventually into Berrien County. As an integral part of their cultural background, these structural values far predated my mother's admonishments. Hence, a hundred years later in the mid-twentieth century, this value code was seen as a solid, long-standing tradition that was never in need of any historical justification. It was simply a logical, cultural practice to be closely adhered to—the light to guide one's daily activities.

Earlier in the chapter entitled *In the Edgware Road*, I noted that the Midwest is perceived by outsiders as being populated by the United States' yeoman farming class. Yeoman is actually a pejorative term used to classify these early Germans (and other non-English-speaking farmers) who, during the nineteenth century, unceremoniously inserted themselves into the various small, Midwest, rural communities among the already present English-speaking residents. These German immigrants were viewed as extremely church- and community-oriented, tradition-bound, plodding, and generally unconcerned with immediate economic gain. To them the land (the farm itself) was, and still is today to most of their direct descendants, a sacred family trust. It is not an object to buy and sell primarily for financial profit. It is to be handed down to their children for it is this piece of ground itself that is the bond that forges the dynamic link between the successive generations.

This ethos has continued unabated in the Middle West for more than a century and a half. It was the ethical foundation upon which my friends and I were raised, although none of us could have ever articulated anything quite so formal. Within the social and environmental context of 80-acre family farms scattered around the regularly spaced small towns of southwestern

Michigan, this ethical foundation has proven to be a successful system of values. It has endured in the Middle West unabated and unchanged over several generations since the mid-nineteenth century.

Be that as it may, we teenagers of Berrien Springs did our share of complaining about having to work, whether on the farm or not. Eighty acres seems large to a young person, and teenagers are notorious for that shirking kind of behavior. We did learn quickly, however, that bellyaching never resulted in rewards and that solid labor could. Hard work and this overwhelming orientation toward future time are Middlewestern standards which derive directly from these early German homesteaders. Today, these moral precepts, particularly the latter, are viewed around the world as the quintessence of the American way of life. It is this specific moral foundation that my undergraduate students consistently translate into the single word "naive."

Upon their arrival in the Middle West, these initial German settlers immediately began buying government land for their farms. The original minimum lot-size purchase permitted for a homestead in 1785 was a square mile (i.e., 640 acres). This was reduced in the early 1800s to 160 acres at $2.00 per acre. A final further reduction occurred in 1820, dropping it down to a quarter section, 80 acres, at $1.25 per acre. Thus, the necessary stage of cheap, available land was set for the massive nineteenth-century German migration into the Middle West. Between 1846 and 1854, more than three million new immigrants arrived in the United States. Of these, about 78 percent were German or Irish. Many of the former continued directly inland from the east coast and settled across the Middle West.

In 1956, one could easily ascertain the early nineteenth-century, Jeffersonian, rural ideal ["Those who labour in the earth are the chosen people of God"—*Notes on the State of Virginia* (1781)] in the 1954 edition of the Berrien County plat book. Here we discover a rural settlement pattern of seemingly self-sufficient nuclear families well entrenched on their 80-acre farmsteads dotting the open countryside of Oronoko Township—Max Calderwood: 80 acres, Frederick Calderwood: 80 acres, Robert Knuth: 80 acres, Edward Berkholz: 80 acres, and Fred Schulz: 80 acres. These are 1/8 of a section. Sometimes these holdings are combined with larger parcels—William H. Schlutt: 160 acres. Other times they are further divided—John Babb: 40 acres and Hugo Heim: 40 acres. Rarer are odd acreage figures—the George

Kephart estate with 55.1 acres, plus two additional, noncontiguous tracts of 40 and 55 acres also listed on the plat map as having been owned by George Kephart.

Land-purchase prices of the mid-nineteenth century, although appearing to be extremely low compared to today's much more inflated standards, put considerable financial strain on the budgets of these new immigrant families. When coupled with the additional heavy initial start-up expenses for tools such as plows, seeds for new crops, and livestock such as cattle, draft horses, and pigs, a farming lifestyle was clearly not a get-rich-quick scheme. Annual return in the beginning was very low, and profits were normally minimal at best. The new farmstead was an investment for the far distant future, thus further reinforcing this basic Midwestern moral value of time that was still to come.

This type of social history was never presented to us in our high school. The descendants of the German settlers had been in our small communities for more than a hundred years and were deeply entrenched. Neither they nor any of the local townspeople saw the need for an annual parade of lederhosen-clad men led down Main Street by an oom-pah band to a Nuhrenberg-style toy shop, there to chug down Bavarian beer from decorated steins. By my generation, they were all just 100 percent American.

Reading through the early local history books, one easily gets the impression that the English speakers were the original effective European settlers in Berrien County—ones to be rapidly followed by the Germans and other northern European immigrants. To the contrary, neither Germans nor New Englanders were the first permanent residents of European extraction in the St. Joseph River Valley. Before them, in the early eighteenth century, a thriving village was built up around the French mission Fort St. Joseph located near Niles. It contained a small community of French fur traders and their families, along with a few priests and some soldiers. In 1720, the Reverend Michael Guignas, a Jesuit, was in charge of spiritual matters for the French residents and members of the military; the local Native Americans who had joined, however minimally, the Catholic Church; and the metis. Father Guignas was joined in leadership by Martin de Montmidy, an officer in the Marine detachment, who handled all of the fort's various military affairs.

For a 53-year period, up to 1773 when the French abandoned the outpost following their defeat in the French and Indian (or

Seven Years) War—the French garrison had already left Fort St. Joseph in 1760—we have access to an extensive baptismal register. It begins in 1720 with this record: "Magdeleine Collet, born the 15th of August, baptized the same day. Died and buried the 8th October, 1720." The notation is signed "M. Guignas of the Soc."[iety of Jesus]. Baptisms were performed for the French, metis, and Native American members of the parish. One entry reads as follows: "In the year 1726 I baptized on the 31st [sic] of april and named vital a son of oucheaghibi [a Native American] about three years old." The presiding priests were also extremely careful to record whether or not the parents were legally married (i.e., in the eyes of God according to Catholic church doctrine): "In the year 1730 the 25th of November I, C M Mesaiger priest and missionary of the society of jesus at the river St joseph, baptized Susanne daughter of Jean baptiste baron resident at the River and of marie Catherine ouekeoukoue of the illinois nation married in the eyes of the church." Hence, we learn that Susanne was the metis offspring of a French father and a Native American mother.

By the 1740s, about 55 French families made their permanent homes around the mission. With the final defeat of France, Fort St. Joseph was abandoned by both the church and the French military. Though the Catholic mission remained in existence for some time, priests were probably not fully administering spiritual help. The last entry in the baptismal record is March 21, 1773. It records the burial of Charles Chevallier, one of the most important Frenchmen in the community. Presiding was Reverend Peter Gibault who, by this date, was one of only three Jesuit priests remaining in the immense territory of France's former western Empire. By 1780, only eight families, 41 persons, remained. The fort was attacked in 1781 by the Spanish and some non-St. Joseph River Potawatomi allies in a hit-and-run raid. The Spanish did not remain to occupy the area. The French settlement completely disappeared from the St. Joseph River Valley in Berrien County and the community seems to have had little or no lasting influence on the surrounding area after that.

Only one name in my high-school yearbook is of probable French extraction: The Calay (Calais?) family was the only Catholic one that I knew in the entire town, but I don't believe they were descendants of the original French settlers of the eighteenth century.

Eating and Drinking

*I*n my cultural diversity class, I ask college students this question: "Why don't we, as Americans, eat cats and dogs?" Amidst their general revulsion at the very thought, they eventually conclude that cats and dogs often assume functional roles as members of our nuclear families and, hence, are almost people like us (and after all, we are not cannibals). These animals have real names, even if they are often descriptive ones such as Spot, Midnight, and Dawg that are not quite human. Dogs may not be completely sacred to us, but they have been labeled as "Man's best friend."

Thus, cats and dogs are more than just pets. Normally, we do not buy them at a "pet store" unless they are rare breeds, but we adopt them from acquaintances who suddenly find themselves with a surplus. Ordinarily their food is purchased at the same time as ours at the supermarket where our pets may have an aisle devoted entirely to themselves. The spatial geography of a typical, modern, large grocery store often dictates that the pet supplies are placed across from, or in the next aisle adjacent to, the baby products. Thus, a supermarket caters indiscriminately to all the members of the family, providing our pets' food, toys, medicines, and the books that will help us to care for and understand them better. The Sunday-newspaper supplements also contain numerous coupons that can be redeemed at the grocery store for our pets' needs. These ads are placed side by side with those for human consumables such as cookies, salad dressing, and cereals. In addition, cat litter and disposable diapers are structural equivalents.

If cats and dogs, then, are not edible foods to think about, Levi-Strauss reminds us that there are still plenty of items in our diet that function as goods to think with. In short, we use food to create conceptual schemes as much as for elegant dining. What has more solemnity for the typical Midwestern, white-American family than a standing rib roast occupying the center of the dining room table? But turn it around: How can one possibly eat beef or any animal for that matter? This is not simply antivivisectionist propaganda because the cow, or the lowly chicken, can be sacred even more so than Fido or Buster. People who believe in voodoo worship may sacrifice chickens, and the Old Testament is replete with instructions on how to properly sacrifice a goat. Yet the former is deemed edible by most white Americans while the latter is rarely on any American menu.

Perhaps more than any human trait other than language, cuisines mark boundaries among cultural groups. Not only do other people eat strange foods, but everyone knows that French cooking is high class though Tibetan might not be. We are what we normally eat: American, French, or Tibetan. Dining out (in a French or Tibetan restaurant) allows us to cross into another cultural realm without traveling very far—sometimes not even beyond the friendly, and safe, confines of our own kitchens.

Culturally speaking, dining out was largely denied to us in southwestern Michigan in the 1950s. We did not have direct access to a host of ethnic restaurants as could have been found in the larger population centers then (though today there is Beijin Palace, Melendez's South of the Border Imports, and the Berrien Springs Oriental Supermarket). Shopping malls where we could sample egg rolls or such ethnic American foods as the pastrami sandwich were still to come. We rarely had the opportunity to cross over into these other worlds. We normally ate at our own table, inside our own house. A summer picnic at Warren Dunes State Park was about as far as we ever went from home to dine.

A typical Sunday dinner in the Hoopingarner household consisted of a wedge (not shredded or pulled apart) of iceberg lettuce drenched with French dressing, a boiled chicken, boiled potatoes (sometimes mashed but more often not), a boiled vegetable such as peas or carrots, white bread with margarine and jam, apple pie, and milk or coffee to drink. In retrospect, that was a pretty plain meal. Except for the apple pie, it was a bland but totally local Midwestern meal for the 1950s. As I think back, there's one curious fact that I can't explain satisfactorily. Despite our heritage, German foods—even the variety of sausages and beer—never were part of our cuisine. Perhaps we were already too Americanized. Seasonings included salt and pepper—never garlic, parsley, sage, rosemary, or thyme. We did not eat spiced foods, and neither did anyone else I knew in town.

This cuisine lacking exotic spices, of course, highlighted the dessert. Desserts were loaded with sugar, and some of them even included nutmeg or cinnamon. Any meal of importance during the week, including supper (the proper term for the evening meal), was a two-stage sequence: all of the dishes except for the sweet, spicy dessert came first as a unit. Then all was removed from the table along with the dirty plates. It was as if the main courses would have been offended at having had to share space with anything so foreign, and clearly non-Midwestern, as nutmeg and cinnamon.

That typical meal contained structures other than the dessert—spice/main courses—no spice binary opposition. One is the manner in which the individual foods are prepared. As a species we begin with a raw item (something natural) and cook it to render it edible. Cooking is thus a cultural transformation of nature.

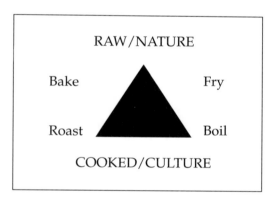

RAW/NATURE

Bake   Fry

Roast   Boil

COOKED/CULTURE

Fire can be applied by either roasting or boiling to affect this transformation. For my Sunday dinner, all of the courses in Phase One that had fire applied to them immediately prior to reaching the table were boiled. Phase Two, the dessert, was baked (roasted). In general, then, dessert-spice-roasted opposes main course-bland-boiled. Here we have a basic Berrien County culinary structure from the 1950s.

Interestingly, even though the specific foods themselves differed, I was greeted with the same structure when I visited my paternal grandmother in western Ohio. The large meal might consist of boiled beef, noodles boiled in the beef broth, and mashed (boiled) potatoes. The same bland rule was in effect, and again all the dishes were carried away from the table before dessert was placed before us. Thus, I could continue to dine comfortably. The dishes differed slightly, but the principles remained the same. I had no cultural adjustments to make.

However, during the big holiday meals, when relatives were present, these rules would seemingly be stood on their heads. Thanksgiving required a roasted (not boiled) turkey with sage dressing. The roasted turkey was served side by side with boiled foods like mashed potatoes, gravy, and vegetables. It was considered safe, in this ritual context of the holiday, to season with sage.

Such meals had other odd features. Relatives were present for dinner, something which seldom happened except on a holiday. People didn't go to their jobs, even though the women still had to work extra diligently in the kitchen. Perhaps strangest of all was the extensive conversation that was carried on around the dinner table. My non-holiday Sunday dinners were accompanied by the barest level of talk, a common feature for many Americans when dinner is not an important social event. In fact, at a normal dinner, all members of the family did not even need to be present if another type of social engagement intervened. I could be, and frequently was, absent from the evening table for sports practices without incurring any social sanctions at home. Holidays obviously demanded contrary, abnormal behavior.

This absentee trend began during the 1920s. The more formal family dinner is now an ancient artifact of American culture, some 70 years or two generations into our own past. Fast-food service industries that have arisen since the 1950s—McDonald's and Burger King, the Chinese take-out, the TV dinner, and even the microwave oven—have reinforced this cultural absenteeism. All of these should have made it easier for the meal to be prepared quickly whenever the family happens by chance to be gathered together; instead, it is now easier for family members to eat on their own whenever they wish. Dining on the run, and running after dining, are now peculiarly and typically American cultural traits.

Despite the family chicken on Sunday—Hoover's promise of a chicken in every pot (for boiling) came true—it was beef that held the highest symbolic value as the one correct American food. This was firmly based on the tradition that we are culturally descended in part from the supreme bull cults of the Middle East, particularly from the Mithraic faith elements which were incorporated into early Christianity. From this ancient religion, Christians borrowed their bull sacrifice, December 25th (the day the sun is reborn), and the bull god. These were structurally transformed into the blood sacrifice of Christ, Christ's birth date, and the devil with his horns and cloven hooves. We now pay homage to the bull as a standing rib roast.

Yet, even back in the mid-nineteenth century while the country's publicists were proudly proclaiming that "America is a nation of beef eaters"—and some people still believe that today—the most consumed red meat of the day was actually pork. Even had this arcane fact been known to them, my family would not have felt enough anxiety to revalue the place of beef in their daily lives. Historical tradition had become a natural fact: as real Americans we needed beef on the table several times a week in order to survive.

On special evenings, but never with relatives in view, we would have sirloin steak. It was always broiled. In the 1950s we never barbecued outside on a grill, a technique that would not become popular or even acceptable for another decade. The steak would be salted, peppered, and have dry, powdered (never fresh mashed and wet) garlic added. Then it would be enclosed in an oven, out of sight, for the cooking. Accompanying this main meat would be baked (not boiled) potatoes. Interestingly, I cannot recall having roast beef until after I had left home.

Rice was seldom eaten. Perhaps it was too foreign, even though it is boiled. When it was served it was only as a dessert, first neutralized by the addition of sugar and milk. Probably acceptability came from this boiling and the safe additions. The most foreign food we ever ate was chop suey—and then only rarely. It was always accompanied by hard Chinese noodles and never by rice on the same plate or even on the table.

Spaghetti was an American dish by the 1950s, yet it had been an acceptable food only since World War I. Prior to that it was strictly an ethnic food clearly delineating Italians from the remainder of the American population. Like the Italians themselves of that earlier era, it was considered low class. It finally reached the American dinner table during the war only after heavy propaganda from the federal government. Large amounts of meat, particularly beef, were required for our fighting men in Europe. Since Italy was our WWI ally, spaghetti's nutritional value was officially recognized for the first time. Together these factors seemingly made it a reasonable substitute for meat and it became a safe item for all Americans regardless of their heritage.

When foods were fried, and this was frequently, it was with lard or butter and almost never with oil. Most certainly not with olive oil—we were of northern and western European descent. Milk products such as cheese, cream, and butter were edible, but olive oil was foreign (i.e., it not only smelled badly, but it also imparted—to us—an unpleasant taste to the food). Its aroma lingered in the air of the house for hours.

Like most Americans, we ate little liver and never kidneys, brains, hearts, or tongue. At that time I only knew that I did not like these cuts (a revulsion of taste), or at least that I should not like them. I had no understanding of the most elementary structuring of these food words. Beef (from the French *boeuf*) and the parts I could eat such as steak and chops were delicious sounding. But tongue, kidney, and heart—terms for organs in my own human body—were distasteful. As with cats and dogs, Berrien County residents were not, and presumably still today are not, cannibals.

Except for Sundays and holidays, the main meal (supper as we normally called it) was always in the evening. I didn't experience a large weekday noontime dinner until 1964 when I was engaged in archeological fieldwork in the Dordogne Valley of France. Few breadwinners in my hometown came back to their houses for lunch, as they typically do in other cultures. The business of America was business (or the farm or the factory), and a big meal at midday would have interrupted the normal routine of earning a living, interfering with what the man of the house was meant to do during the daylight hours. To this day, I still can't eat a hefty meal at noon; and if I tarry in conversation at lunch with anyone, my conscience urges me to stop wasting time and to get back to work.

Certain holidays and the rare family gatherings might be true social events which included uncharacteristic conversation. Yet, compared with, say, Hispanic cultures, there was a great difference. After Thanksgiving dinner was over, the men retired immediately to the living room to smoke and watch football. The ritual viewing of the game, a totally passive response, would be equally intermixed with, or even dominated by, the active response of actually talking to someone about something. The genders were totally separated, and the children would be off somewhere else. A minimal age/gender status grading rule was in effect.

Excepting holidays, we rarely, if ever, ate with other families in a home setting. Being invited to dinner at the Sherwoods or the Baloughs, as a social event, was not a part of our cultural lexicon. Besides, what would our parents have talked about? We might ask a friend of mine to stay for dinner, but would not have thought to include his parents. They were probably having the same things for dinner anyway—meat and potatoes. Further, if someone prepared some new cuisine, nontraditional dishes for the Midwest such as tacos with a dreaded hot sauce, he or she would have been seen as strange or, worse, uppity.

However, we might join other family members and some friends for a holiday picnic, particularly on July 4. These ritual summer occasions took place on the Lake Michigan beach at Warren Dunes. The fare would include the usual hot dogs, hamburgers, potato salad, and covered dishes. A swim in Lake Michigan was required followed by a picnic meal. Finally, we would climb and roll down the dunes, inviting hills of sand, until we were exhausted and starving again. I have not spent much time on a lake beach since those days, but the sight of sand usually stimulates my appetite.

By way of contrast, in Hispanic cultural dinner gatherings—as with some other cultures—everyone and all the dirty dishes remain to the end. Nothing distracts them from the conversation, and members of both genders participate freely. This can continue for hours, long after the food has been eaten. This contrast with Hispanic culture shows why so many Americans, including myself, make such poor dinner guests in other cultural settings. It is not that we are insensitive to proper behavior. It is more that we think we already know how to behave at dinner: eat quickly, converse little, and get on about your business (TV, homework, the evening paper, mowing the lawn, and so on). Remaining at a table littered with leftovers and dirty dishes after the eating process is complete is not good manners. We learn that fact in our highchairs and seldom, if ever, stop following that cultural proscription.

Even though I couldn't have structured my own diet then, and I never thought much about it, a certain group in town did eat differently. These were the Seventh-day Adventists who arrived in Berrien Springs with the construction of Emmanuel Missionary College in 1901. Not only did they worship in what seemed a totally unorthodox manner—sundown Friday to sundown Saturday—but their diet set them apart most clearly. They didn't place any value on red meat—many of them never ate any at all—and most certainly not pork, heeding as they did the abominations of Leviticus and conceding that the original diet of Adam and Eve in the Garden of Eden was strictly vegetarian. Since many of them were vegetarians, we were convinced that they viewed us with considerable distaste because we were not. Long before soy products became a "hip" food in the outside world, my Adventist neighbors were eating "choplets" for dinner. I learned to stay well clear of their houses at this time of day because I found the odor overpowering and quite unpleasant.

This was my initial introduction to the cuisine of the cultural other. It varied just enough from mine to be recognizable. The Adventists did nothing outwardly strange with fruits and vegetables, many of which they grew themselves on their well-tended farms. They simply did not partake of red meat. And except for worshipping on Saturday, they still generally dressed, looked, and spoke English as we did. Yet, I was aware that they were not us because we knew what was good to eat and they did not.

The Adventists had their food taboos, most specifically one against pork, and we had ours, too. Of course, we were not aware of them as formal proscriptions. Certainly, we were not cannibals; and we did not eat bugs, worms, or snakes either, obviously because they were not good for us. I didn't know why the Other wouldn't eat pork. It seemed silly. Despite semi-regular attendance at Methodist Sunday School, I was not yet aware of the abominations of Leviticus (11:4-7) where it was proscribed that the camel, hare, rock badger, and pig were off-limits for both eating and sacrificing. Even if I had been cognizant of this fact, it wouldn't have made much sense to me. We never overtly participated in any ritual sacrificing of any animals, and it never would have occurred to us to eat either camels or, except on a lark, anything similar to a ground hog. For my own subsequent mental development, it is undoubtedly fortunate that I did not inquire into the matter. What would I have made of the conclusion that pork is taboo because the pig has a cloven hoof but does not chew its cud? The camel, hare, and rock badger are to be avoided because they chew their cud but do not have a cloven hoof. (Hares and rock badgers twitch their noses, a behavior that, in the eyes of some early naturalists several millennia ago, apparently simulated cud chewing.)

Anthropologists have been fascinated for decades with the ways that cuisines and food taboos have been employed to create group boundaries. If a group classifies all the mammals in its world according to the presence and/or absence of cud chewing and cloven hoofs, we have only four possible categories: both traits present, both absent, or one present and the other absent. The landscape within which the Old Testament was written contained ten mammals with both characteristics: sheep and goats (both wild and domesticated), cattle, and five species of deer and antelope. These were all animals that were normally eaten. Ninety species of mammals lacked both traits including all of the carnivores, horses, and many others, not forgetting humans; none of these typically were found on the dinner table.

The camel, hare, rock badger, and pig are clearly anomalous and defied simple classification using these two criteria alone. Thus, they required special symbolic consideration—one verse each in Leviticus where they are deemed unclean, both for eating and sacrificing. Their ban for ritual sacrifice was equally important since, as we learn from the Old Testament, this was an important act up until after the construction of the first temple. The sacrificed animals were then redistributed and eaten.

The pig stands out even more starkly when we remember that the prime enemies of the newly emerging State of Israel were the Canaanites. Not only did the Canaanites eat pigs, but pigs also served as their key ritual animal. The pig taboo was a concept that Moses had learned while still in Egypt, one that he carried with him on the Exodus. In this historical context, we can understand how pig avoidance provided a basic symbolic separation between these two contending groups. The pig taboo is one of the many factors that has allowed the Jewish people to maintain their identity for millennia. Thus, the tradition of the unclean pig has a history long predating its acceptance and present-day observance by my childhood neighbors, the Seventh-day Adventists.

The family of one of my classmates, Kenneth Peters, owned a goat farm. How they made a living is still an enduring mystery to me. Nobody that I knew drank goat's milk or ate goat meat. In fact, goat meat is largely avoided (though not a formal taboo) among most white Americans even today. I never questioned this avoidance, nor any food taboos, within the context of what I was learning in Sunday School about foods and the Old Testament. In fact, I cannot recall that Leviticus was ever mentioned. I suspect that these types of mental gymnastics would have been lost on a 16-year-old boy. The Adventists simply were different. They did not eat the same things that we did, and it was enough to know that dining with them would always be an uncomfortable experience—one to be avoided at all costs. When my friend Eddie Lugenbeal's mother started frying choplets, I always fled—as if the Devil were hot on my tail—across the street to my home and the sweet smell of boiling potatoes.

Until I went away to the University of Michigan, I knew no other vegetarians. All of my friends ate red meat. I thought that vegetarianism was simply a quaint custom followed by no one else in the world except Seventh-day Adventists. I had seen many animals killed and butchered and had participated in these acts myself, but I was unable to imagine that this might offend anyone to the point of not eating red meat. My friends and their families regularly had beef or pork on the table, often from their own home-grown livestock. They all felt as I did: meat taboos are unnatural. Or, as I might better phrase it today, all food—including meat taboos—involves highly cultural acts.

Our dining included another oddity. We seldom ever ate in restaurants except on a long day trip to, say, Chicago. Berrien Springs had two cafés, the Shamrock and the Green Lantern, but I don't recall anyone I knew eating an evening meal in either of them. Perhaps an acquaintance would have breakfast, coffee and doughnuts, or, even more rarely, a light lunch; but everyone went home for supper, normally at five o'clock.

The Shamrock, one of two cafés in town.

Shops in town, including the Green Lantern.

We had no McDonald's or Burger King for fast foods. The first McDonald's I remember, in South Bend in 1958, proudly proclaimed "almost 1,000,000 sold" and "a hamburger, fries, a coke, and change for a dollar." Pizza had just entered the local scene, with one pizzeria in St. Joseph. Both McDonald's and the pizzeria were too new for us to have settled into any ceremonial behavior in our approach to them. Today a meal at McDonald's is a ritual experience. The building itself with its Golden Arches is as distinctive and easily recognizable as a Mormon Church in the Peruvian Andes where Catholicism holds sway. One assumes a certain, but unconscious, demeanor before entering, just as we do prior to stepping into our own churches.

We had, instead, Henderson's Drive-In with its female car hops and superb root beer. Here we gathered by the carload for hours on evenings from April to October. Walking over, even across the street from our school athletic park Sylvester Field, was out of the question. We had to eat and drink while sitting in a car or pick-up truck, not on a bench or at a picnic table. The car hops—clean, healthy, teenage girls—wore identical costumes and expected certain forms of behavior from us. We never inquired about prices or what was on the menu; we already possessed that basic knowledge.

In other words, the conversation, as well as our actions, were embedded in a culturally prescribed litany; and both car hops and customers recited the invocations and responses appropriately. The window tray and root beer mugs never varied in style, and neither did the flavors of the drinks or the taste of the hamburgers. The act of eating was accompanied by semi-lewd remarks directed at the car hops who sometimes replied in kind; and this, too, was expected. Finally, with the meal over and the tray removed, engines were revved up and gravel was spit and sprayed by tires as we made our exit. This ceremonial observance is one that never varied. It was as comfortable as a root beer on a hot afternoon, and, like all of our other dining rituals, was completely unrecognized as such by us.

We seldom visited either of the local cafes, except the Shamrock with its pinball machine. The soda fountains, of which there were two, both in drug stores, were another matter. Soda fountains are no longer a part of American life. I doubt that many teenagers today, at least those in larger towns and cities, have heard of them, much less spent time on a stool at the counter. We invested hours at what we knew as Chamberlain's (officially filed as Schug's Drugs in 1966), on the corner of Main and Ferry, and lesser amounts of time at Krause's, just westward down the block on Ferry Street.

To be a soda jerk in those days was to occupy a status position of some importance. The mixing of coke or soda water and a flavoring (a phosphate) was a true art form. Where can one purchase a cherry phosphate today? Both of our local soda fountains produced excellent chocolate malteds (not milk shakes!), matched in my memory only by a single emporium found in Shoshoni, Wyoming. We loitered, read magazines off the rack, and talked while sitting at the counter or in a booth and nursing a single nickel coke. In bad weather, we milled around aimlessly inside; during the summer months, we wandered back and forth to and from the outside. These soda fountains were also air conditioned, a rarity in our town in 1956. They were, in essence, the structural equivalent of today's shopping malls, and the cokes and malteds were not incidental to dreaming.

I have come to learn that our cuisines play a crucial role in how our lives are structured. More than simply foods to nourish our bodies, the array of dishes, preparations, and status positions—from chief chef to soda jerk—input messages to us daily. Three square meals, meat and potatoes, and week-night dinners at 5:30 p.m. were more than mere habits; they became integral segments of my boyhood ritual behavior. And while it was (and still is) legitimate to upset these segments on Thanksgiving or the Fourth of July, to do so on July 2 or October 10 was to challenge the natural order of the universe. Understanding dawned not through dining with Turks or Latins, but through realizing that what we consider to be natural is first and foremost cultural. If the goat possesses both cloven hoofs and cud chewing as biological attributes and is a suitable offering to the Lord in sacrifice, then it just might be edible.

Children in the Foliage

One distinct advantage to growing up in Berrien County not normally afforded to small-town young people everywhere was an early exposure to what is labeled today in anthropology as the "cultural other." The majority of the population of Berrien Springs, and the county in general, was of western European background. But I was completely aware that there were differences, both genetic and cultural, among the people I might see daily. However, I never utilized this fact for positive learning. My advantage, after all, came long before any true sensitivity to cultural and ethnic diversity was being promoted in the United States as a whole. At mid century, we still struggled mightily under the oppressive weight of the "melting pot" ideology, a social theory that has been largely, and appropriately in my opinion, discarded by scholars today.

Courses in social studies and history at my high school concentrated almost exclusively on the world of free, white, and usually male Americans. Thus, for most of the small-town teenagers of my generation, the sole exposure to this "cultural other" was through the *National Geographic Magazine*, particularly the "African pictures" of partially naked women dancing among warriors brandishing spears in an open, central plaza surrounded by thatched-roof huts. These graphic images usually served to set in stone our future cultural attitudes toward these people—even those, such as the African Americans, actually residing within our own midst. The magazine provided ready-made cultural traditions and perceptions—ones that were patently false, but ones that we could never see clearly around much less through.

All societies have some kind of status grading, even if it is only minimal age and gender ranking. The Berrien Springs of my youth was no exception. It was obvious to me that differences existed among people and groups, of course, but I couldn't have articulated what made them stand apart from us except in the most basic of ways. Because of their skin color, we thought the African Americans were lower class (as not only a kind of mis-understood genetic programing but also undoubtedly from what we thought we had learned about their cultural heritage in the *National Geographic*). We believed likewise about southern white migrants—due, probably, to their slow, drawling speech patterns, their normal occupation as itinerant farm workers, and their general overall nomadic lifestyle. All of this cultural and biological variability was starkly obvious to us and formed a reservoir from which we could draw at will for the purpose of group formation and, hence, ultimately for misguided ethnic and social status classifications.

About as close as we high-school students ever came consciously to "the other" on a daily basis was our annual German exchange student. (We did have one foreign refugee resident, Guntis Vitums. He and his mother had escaped from Latvia, leaving the father behind, but he never talked about his homeland, his father, or his past.) Every year a young male student came from Germany to spend the academic year with us. Victor King, who tripled as our guidance counselor, social studies teacher, and German instructor, had spent World War II in Germany. He initiated this student-exchange program upon beginning his career at our high school. Our senior year the student was Peter Krawutsehke from Karlsruhe. I do not remember ever questioning Pete, or any other exchange student for that matter, on life in his homeland. We were never pushed to do so, and hence their presence among us stands simply as another lost opportunity for learning.

Directly across the street from me lived my frequent playmate Eddie Lugenbeal. His mother was my piano teacher. He was a Seventh-day Adventist. At that time the local Adventists numbered in the hundreds. They used the old 1839 Court House—a wooden temple-front Greek Revival building with four showy fluted Doric columns built in 1838-1839—both as a church and a secondary-level school. Since they shared their parking lot with the public school, we were aware of their presence every day.

Only a small minority of their population lived within the immediate confines of the town limits. Most of them resided on or near the Emmanuel Missionary College campus north of town. The greatest percentage of them I never knew, and they did not interact heavily, at least on a social basis, with most of the townspeople. In dress, overall public demeanor, and everyday language, they were normally unrecognizable and, hence, generally invisible to outsiders. Nonetheless, they were still a persistent social enclave among us.

It is unfortunate that I never received any instruction concerning exactly how they differed from us. I knew that, even though they went to church on Saturday, oddly enough they believed in God and Jesus. Still, the structure and esoterica of their religious beliefs were never explained to me and remained an enduring mystery to me throughout my boyhood. How and when the Adventists happened to find their way to Berrien Springs and, more explicitly, who the Adventists were, never seemed to matter much to anyone around me, at least not enough to expound upon them.

Their name comes from their belief that Saturday, and not Sunday, is the true Sabbath (Genesis 2:1-3 and Exodus 20:8-11) and that the second coming (the Advent) of Christ is imminent. The believers organized as a union in 1863, partly with the help of James White (1821-1881) and his wife, Ellen Harmon White (1827-1915). They amalgamated several existing sects of adherents into one functioning and dynamic religious and social unit.

Part of their belief system is traceable to William Miller (born in upstate New York in 1782). The early- and mid-nineteenth century in the United States witnessed considerable religious ferment within the context of heavy immigration and its attendant social

James and Ellen White

and spiritual upheavals. (Between 1846 and 1854 over three million immigrants came to the United States, most of them of German or Irish background.) One movement was championed by Miller who preached a doctrine predicting the immediate return of Christ. On the basis of his biblical studies, particularly his analysis of Daniel 8, Miller prophesied that the Advent would take place between March 21, 1843, and March 21, 1844. When it failed to materialize, Miller recalculated Christ's return for October 22, 1844. Again, he and his followers were disappointed.

Mrs. White made important contributions to Adventist theology through her confirming visions of distinctive doctrines. Shortly after Joseph Bates introduced her to the seventh-day Sabbath in 1846, she received a vision confirming its truth. Similarly, during a conference in 1848, she experienced a vision attesting to the truth of Hiram Edson's "sanctuary doctrine," first published in 1845. Edson had proposed that the cleansing of the sanctuary in Daniel 8:14—which Miller had interpreted as Jesus' coming to cleanse the earth—actually referred to the heavenly sanctuary alluded to in Hebrews 8-9. Therefore, in Edson's and subsequently White's view, Adventists had been mistaken in regard to the event which had taken place on October 22, 1844. Rather than returning to earth, Jesus had entered a new phase of his priestly ministry. Thus, the reliance on a specific date for the forthcoming Advent was removed, but the official doctrine could still be grounded empirically on received scripture. With this cleansing of the heavenly sanctuary now completed, the final phase of Earth's history was said to have begun.

On October 1, 1860, in nearby Battle Creek, Michigan, and with the Whites' support, the official name for the new denomination became the Seventh-day Adventist Church. Their first institute of higher education, Battle Creek College, was established in 1874. After the turn of the century, it was moved to Berrien Springs. By 1956, the school could boast 942 students from 21 foreign countries and 36 states. Today, the Seventh-day Adventist Church numbers over ten million strong and is rapidly growing through their highly successful, world-wide missionary movement.

Seventh-day Adventists envision the world as witnessing a constant struggle between Christ and the Devil, with God as the ultimate and final Judge. Each person is responsible for making his or her own decision to join the forces of either good or evil. A person's acts do not affect his or her own (or anyone else's) chances for salvation. Righteousness comes through accepting Christ as

Emmanuel Missionary College around 1950.

Savior and results in concrete, everyday, moral behavior.

The Adventists are a law-abiding and decidedly nonrevolutionary sect. Mrs. White herself wrote that "He who obeys the Divine Law will truly respect and obey the laws of his country." The church thus provides a clear and specific moral position toward all secular affairs.

This is undoubtedly why we had so much difficulty goading Seventh-day Adventist young people into actions they found morally repugnant. We were actually extremely dangerous to their futures as individuals and hence to the fate of their very souls. We would drive out to their campus and engage in name calling and other rowdy actions, such as hurling squashes or pumpkins at them from speeding cars. But they never responded in kind. The college students always remained completely calm and outwardly unmoved by our beastly behavior.

Our way of life did not correspond with their understanding of the construction of the universe. We worshipped on Sunday. We smoked, drank, danced, fought, and used profane language. We must have been excellent instructors for their youth as models of what real evil and temptation were like in everyday life. It is no wonder that they avoided us. All of these actions and many more that we engaged in daily are explicitly proscribed. God asks of them (and of all of us) careful attention to morality.

On only one occasion did I ever witness a failure among them. One spring night we were using their excellent college library to prepare our high-school term papers. When we emerged from the building, we ran into a hostile crowd hassling an African American male student and a white girl. With them was a classmate of ours, a "fallen" Adventist in fact, who was busily defending them. Apparently the couple had been seen too often in each other's company, and the crowd was conveying a warning of their disapproval. Our friend didn't necessarily care about the African American student, and neither did we, but the situation created an opportunity for a potential fight and we seized it gladly. Nothing developed beyond a little shouting and shoving, but even that was uncharacteristic of the Adventists. Today I find no satisfaction with this rout and regret having been involved at all.

As a youth I had very little direct interaction with Seventh-day Adventists in the business arena. I do not recall any direct criticism of how they handled themselves in the world of finance. I had all I could manage with my own less-than-one-dollar-a-week spending allowance. I think they were perceived by the townspeople as honest, scrupulous, and totally trustworthy in all areas. This is exactly the image of themselves that they wish to project, and in this they were highly successful. They were a model I should have emulated myself.

When they first arrived in 1901, the Seventh-day Adventists were welcomed with smiles and open arms. They immediately began constructing buildings for their college north of town while renting the 1839 Court House for a church and school. They continued to occupy this structure until 1966. By 1956, having prospered despite a lack of significant interaction with the town as a whole, they had become socially marginal to Berrien Springs' citizenry. Even the lower class, which was obviously the majority of the townsfolk, could look down on them. And, unfortunately, they did. The Adventists provided an opportunity for status grading that was readily acceptable to most of the locals. Thus, by 1956, despite the fact that in 1901 they had been greeted eagerly, the social order of the town appeared to have more than a half a century of structural tradition behind it. A contemporary cultural practice had become a perfectly natural, logical, and seemingly historically based behavior.

Although there may have been several, I personally knew of

The 1839 Court House being used as a church and a school.

only one interfaith marriage. The wife was an Adventist, and the husband was not. They lived away from the campus in the opposite direction well south of town across the St. Joseph River. He was a milk man and a Little League baseball coach. For the small remuneration of about a dollar a day, I occasionally helped him in the summer on his deliveries early in the morning. His route included Benton Harbor, so considerable driving was involved and we had much time for talking. His main complaint, and an incessant one at that, was the complete absence of meat on the dinner table. For him, as a true Midwesterner, a main evening meal without meat was not a proper dinner.

One section of his route I normally completed by myself, as he had a daily visit to make. We would park down the street, and he would leave milk bottles up to a certain house, and there he would go inside. I would continue, collecting the empties and dropping off full bottles of milk, cream, and half-and-half, and then return to the truck and read for awhile. I still don't believe his explanation that he was merely having a roast beef sandwich for a mid-morning snack. I did, nonetheless, conclude that given my own dietary peculiarities, a Seventh-day Adventist woman most likely wouldn't be in my future.

If the Adventists melted in as far as appearance, the members of the House of David (the Israelites) did not. Today, the males' long flowing hair and full beards would not necessarily seem out of place. But in 1956, an era of crew cuts and clean-shaven faces, they were clearly visible. They arrived in Benton Harbor in 1903, just two years after the Seventh-day Adventists, under the leadership of Benjamin Franklin Purnell (1861-1927). However, the Israelites did not receive an enthusiastic welcome. In his *History of Benton Harbor and Tales of Village Days* (1915), James Pender recounts that one local newspaper, the *Expositor*, headlined a critical article on the House of David (or Flying Rollers as it referred to them) with this title: "Kill the Frauds."

Like the Adventists, the Israelites were vegetarians, believed the second coming was near at hand, and were anxiously anticipating the Ingathering of the twelve tribes (the 144,000 prophesied in Revelation). But, in contrast to the Adventists, they celebrated working and living communally, espoused celibacy, and preached the salvation of both the soul and the youthful body (Job 33:23-25). Hence, they stood out both culturally and visually.

King Ben, as my family and many others usually referred to him, was born in Kentucky. Early in life he developed a love for preaching and fell in with the Jezreelites, another Millennium Age sect. On March 12, 1895, he proclaimed himself to be the Seventh Messenger, succeeding the Sixth Messenger James J. Jezreel (the first was Joanna Southcott of Devonshire, England, in 1792).

Despite obvious cultural differences, Purnell made the House of David a positive economic force in Berrien County. They were

Israelites of the House of David.

deeply involved in a very successful agriculture enterprise, owning several farms throughout the region as well as a cold storage plant and the largest open-air, non-citrus market in the world. They promoted a variety of tourist ventures. I remember best the miniature trains and cars at their Eden Springs amusement park in Benton Harbor where we would travel on a summer's evening to eat ice cream, play, and stare at the oddly visaged Israelites who worked at the facility. And, of course, I remember their excellent baseball team. I saw them perform dozens of times and can still see the players' beards and long hair flying as they ran the bases or chased a blue darter in the outfield.

I knew nothing about their history or their religious beliefs in 1956 beyond the fact that they had forsaken sex. As a hormone-driven teenager, I could neither understand nor countenance that odd behavior. I was also unaware that there were two factions, the original House of David having been rendered asunder in 1928. Following Purnell's trial and conviction as a religious imposter in 1927 (but not as a seducer of young girls as it was widely thought by their unbelieving, gossiping neighbors) and his death a month later, his widow, Mary, and his closest confidant, Judge Harry T. Dewhirst, split the colony in two. Each faction gathered up followers and property. Though Mary's faction retained most of the star baseball players, both sides had the teams that so enralled me, and Dewhirst's group received Eden Springs.

The House of David owned two separate properties in or near Berrien Springs in 1956. I was completely unaware of both of them. One—Rocky Farm—lay at the south end of Lake Chapin between Range Line Road and the St. Joseph River at the end of Rocky Road. The farm plat book for 1954 lists the property as including 318.67 acres; it was awarded to Judge Dewhirst's faction in the final settlement. Interestingly, adjacent to the south is another farm of 152 acres listed as "Mary Purnell Tr."; Mary, herself, died on August 19, 1953. Yet, despite the presence of these two farms within the confines of Oronoko Township, I never saw a member of the House of David on the streets of Berrien Springs. Within the city limits of Berrien Springs was Maryland Farm which was also awarded to Mary's group. Since 1947 the land has been the site of the Berrien County Youth Fair and the Berrien Springs public schools. This fact was, in 1956, nowhere formally commemorated by the town.

A smaller religious group on the fringes of the town's mainstream were the Pentecostals. Their church was located above the post office on Ferry Street. Their clientele consisted mainly of first and second generation southerners who had come to the area, most likely as migrant workers, and who later chose to remain. Some of their children attended school with me, usually dropping out at the legal age of 16, but I do not know how much of Berrien County was drawn upon for their membership. I certainly did not recognize most of the congregation.

Their services were not muted and quiet, but rather exuberant. Loud music was accompanied by innumerable hallelujahs and amens. I did not in those days view this as a joyous celebration of their faith in God; instead, I interpreted it as one that was exceedingly raucous and undignified, rather like a rock concert dedicated to the Lord. One service was held every Thursday night. A group of us teenage boys would stand listening across the street. Although we could not see the service itself, we could eavesdrop when their windows were open. We would snicker, and, I think, imagine along with them the visions of hell's fires and brimstone that were being depicted in the sermon.

For the most part, they, too, were a marginal social group to whom most of the townspeople could feel superior. They were largely poor, not well educated by our standards, held the lowest paying jobs, and occupied a lower rung of the town's social ladder. They appeared to us boys to have little ambition to make something of their lives, although this is almost certainly untrue. I feel sure that had we ever asked them what they wanted from life, we would not have understood them anyway. For them life was exceedingly difficult, and this is certainly reflected in their one major solace, their religious beliefs. It was their faith in God and heaven's rewards that enabled them to endure all of their manifold hardships and tribulations.

Not all of the southerners were Pentecostals. Some had integrated, at least partially, into the overall social fabric of the town, though often deemed unworthy of higher status. My own father, Lester (Jake), was of southern descent through his father Jacob, originally out of Louisiana. My father had migrated northward from western Ohio around 1939, fleeing, I am told, a bad gambling debt. He took a job at Clark Equipment Company running a drill press and rented a room at my grandmother's boarding house where he met my mother.

Other southerners, but non-Pentecostals, included two brothers (fraternal twins) who were in my graduating class (and one sister who was also a classmate but who dropped out of school before our senior year). The family had originally come to Berrien Springs from Arkansas around 1950. I was never especially close to them, but we were friends. I was in their house several times and ate at their table.

More readily identifiable at a distance were the African Americans and Hispanics (most probably Chicanos) who came to Berrien County during the summer to find labor as migrant workers. My yearbook for 1958 lists 245 high-school students. Of these, only Linda and William Lewis, both Freshmen, were African American. I do not remember either one of them, and I have no idea if they remained to graduate with their peers.

We had virtually no opportunity to interact with African Americans except on the farm. Even in Benton Harbor where a large number of them were permanent residents, they were not heavily employed in any of the shops that I was likely to visit with my mother. I was the same age as Chet Walker who was a marvelous basketball player. He later went on to Bradley University and National Basketball Association fame. Our high-school team played several games against him, and we lost them all quite convincingly. But I never was at a single social gathering with him, and we never interacted off of the basketball court.

We occasionally had African American students in our class, but they seemed to attend for only a few months. Then they disappeared. I do not know how they felt about us, but I cannot remember any nasty racial incidents emanating from my friends. However, I suspect that we did not make them feel overly welcome even if we did not tease and taunt them. We weren't necessarily unaware of segregation in its larger sense. I think we just didn't feel threatened by them in any way, perhaps because they weren't around long enough to ever make a lasting impression upon us.

One aged African American man we did know, and we visited him selfishly and rather frequently. For the price of a bottle of the cheapest rot-gut wine, he would go to the local grocery store and purchase a case of beer for us. We would roar up to the door of his shack near Eau Claire late at night and yell for him to come out. Sometimes he invited us in, and there we viewed real poverty. His wife, Mary, invariably disapproved of his service, but off he would go with us.

I don't remember a single Hispanic in my high school. I saw

them on the streets or in the stores during the harvest seasons and could hear them speaking Spanish in public. This, alone, seemed rather dangerous to me. Who could know what or whom they were talking about or foresee what plans they were laying that might bring no future good for the town? Until bilingualism becomes valued, language is and remains a major barrier among cultures.

I only had one opportunity as a youth to spend time with any Hispanics. My Uncle Herb employed some migrant workers on his farm. One of the children was a girl my age. It was the only time in my life that I volunteered for farm labor; whatever job she had, I was sure to join her. One morning she came out of their cabin, her black hair freshly washed and shining. I followed her to the asparagus picker and off we went with my uncle driving. After a few minutes, one of her younger brothers nudged me and reached down and picked up a clod of wet earth. With a perfect hook-shot motion, he hurled this muddy package into the air. It landed squarely on her head. It was the first time I ever witnessed the famed Latin temper. It was only years later, after living among Latinos for two decades, that I actually learned the meaning of some of the words I heard that morning. A few days after the incident, the Hispanics moved on; and much to my great heartache, they never returned.

For me, all these people were without a history. With a little investment of time and some sensitivity I could have learned something of the past of the Adventists or the House of David, but it never dawned on me that they might have pasts or that I might find them interesting. The Native Americans had no true pasts in 1956, at least none that were officially acknowledged by the outside power structure which to me was our school system and my elders. They did not publicize what they knew about themselves and their own history. At best, we as outsiders are only now rediscovering their story through archeological and ethnohistoric research in my own generation. It was never truly lost to them. Further, much of what we propose to Native American groups concerning their own individual pasts is often entirely unintelligible, and, just as frequently, quite irrelevant to them. We can create and propose accurate reconstructions of how it was from the outsider's view, but we cannot always convince "the other" to take us seriously.

An Antique Drum

*I*n the minds of my high-school friends and me, nothing was at all revolutionary about our daily attire. Clothes were an uncomplicated affair both for me and for most of my male class-mates. The colors of my various articles of clothing matched only by accident (and still do so today). I can't remember that we ever worried much about high-class style in any larger sense. What we may have considered the current fashion rage was across the ocean in Paris, in New York City, or—much closer to home—in Chicago. All were urban types of garments and we normally avoided them at all cost.

For the most part, what we knew about more foreign, non-American styles of dress we learned from the *National Geographic Magazine* or through the *Movietone* newsreels during the Saturday matinee at the Berry Theater—our sole, and well-frequented, local movie house. The latter information came to us mainly as unique *cine veritie* featuring skinny, and apparently upper-class, fashion models parading around on a stage at some fancy boutique in Paris in what we usually considered to be really ugly clothing. No sane person would actually wear those outfits in public—or so we generally preferred to believe.

We did have our own styles, of course. Certain items of dress were defined as cool and, hence, publicly wearable, while others we would never be seen dead in, much less cavort around in up and down the hallways of the high school. Thus we dressed according to the proper fashion of with-it teenagers.

Guys all wore Levis, sport shirts with muted colors, and boots, moccasins, or sneakers every day. In the summer, shirts were short-sleeved; in the winter, they were long-sleeved with the cuffs rolled up twice. The top two buttons of the shirt were left

103

open. Collars were always arranged to stand up straight along the back of the neck. Baseball caps were popular in the summer; but, unlike the present day, they were never allowed in the classroom. And we never wore a hat of any kind in the winter, at least not after we were out of sight of our mothers.

Dress suits were definitely not cool, but each boy owned at least one. Mine always seemed to be very dark blue or brown in color; charcoal gray would have been much preferred and more appropriate for a 1950s teenager. These good suits were worn with ties and heavily starched white shirts to church on Sunday and to the more formal high-school dances. We never would have been seen wearing any suit—or even a good pair of slacks, if we could possibly help it—within the confines of the high school during a normal day. Suits were acceptable at certain dances only because we saw other teenage boys so adorned every weekday afternoon on Dick Clark's *American Bandstand* which first went on the air in August of 1957. Since few of us could actually dance to rock-and-roll music without embarrassment, we spent most of our time at these supposedly festive occasions shuffling uncomfortably, but well-dressed, around the sidelines of the gymnasium.

Suits were also necessary for one of our prime Saturday-night activities during the winter—wedding receptions held at the Baroda American Legion Hall nearly every weekend. We attended them faithfully, even though we rarely knew either the bride or the groom. Sometimes we were not even aware of their names by the time we staggered out the door for home. To have worn Levis would have been entirely inappropriate. We most likely would have been refused entry into the building and, hence, would have had no access to the food and free-flowing keg beer that had drawn us there in the first place.

We boys very rarely wore shorts, even in the summer. Shorts were reserved, or so it seems to me now, for the gymnasium or basketball practice. We did appreciate girls in shorts—the shorter the better of course; but teenage boys in those days in Berrien County were not much given to showing off their legs (and simultaneously exposing themselves to the mocking taunts of even their closest friends). Comfortable, sensible Levis not only completely covered one's lower limbs, but they also were perfectly acceptable for work, play, most dates, and, of course, all high-school classes. We could walk around—winter and summer alike—knowing that we were properly dressed for almost all events and occasions, excluding those that were considered by our parents to be the most ceremonial in nature.

During my senior year, (outrageous) pink pants were apparently the fashion rage somewhere (probably in the East or maybe in southern California). One morning a student arrived at school wearing a pair of these monstrosities. After a few extremely nasty comments on our part, he slipped out the door, returned rapidly home, and changed back into his Levis. It was a fad that never took hold with us. On another occasion, a classmate came to school wearing a pair of trousers that were held up by an elastic waistband rather than a perfectly serviceable, leather belt. While he was removing books from his locker, with his back carelessly turned toward us, another guy unceremoniously yanked his pants to the floor, exposing both white jockey shorts and whiter bare thighs. Again, we were spared having to emulate these bizarre fashions of the outside world.

I don't believe we ever worried about tanning. In 1956, this sun-worshipping ritual had not yet filtered down to those of us who lived in small Middle Western towns. Thus, we were not required to spend an inordinate number of hours lying greased-up and immobile on a towel in our backyards or on the beach along Lake Michigan at Warren Dunes, accomplishing nothing beyond frying our brains and bodies. For boys, tanned arms and faces came from swimming or playing baseball. No contests ensued to see who could achieve the brownest skin during the summer, an act which would have made shorts mandatory. While working on the farm, we stayed relatively blocked from direct rays with hats, trousers, and long-sleeved shirts. A farmer's tan on only the backs of the hands and neck along with the lower face was a common sight. Such full-field attire offered protection not only from the sun but also from the hay and straw produced during haying and threshing in the fields. (Making hay is probably the most odious work ever invented.) We were not worried about skin cancer, which was relatively unknown to us then. Hence, tanning was never a topic of much concern to any of us. In fact, tanning as a serious cultural activity had not become a truly popular pastime in the United States until the mid-1930s and then only initially among the upper class. (Commercially manufactured tanning lotions were first put on the market in 1935.) Before then, a white person whose skin was burnt dark signified, as it still does today in many third-world countries such as in Latin America, that the person spends considerable time engaged in hard manual labor outdoors—obviously not an upper-class preoccupation. In that particular cultural context, the darker you are, the lower your social status. This is one form of color symbolism that has been partly stood upon its head in the United States during the intervening forty years. In the 1950s, golden-bronzed skin simply did not have the cultural value it has enjoyed since.

Generally, I was unaware of any cultural code pertaining to one's attire. I vaguely knew, of course, that night clothes (pajamas, for example, which I never wore) opposed day wear (Levis), and that one should dress up (a suit) for church and dress down (Levis) for play or work. But these were, as they have to be, normally unarticulated rules. It was also obvious to me that denim, which in 1956 I didn't know was manufactured from cotton, was coarser than silk and that one would never manufacture a suit or a party dress from denim. I did have that much of a sense of what style was all about.

It was in 1958 when I blissfully arrived in Ann Arbor that I first learned not only that were there some definite rules but also that I had no idea what they might be. All my male freshman peers wore dress slacks to class; some even wore suits and ties. In my dormitory, South Quad, was one young man we called Animal. His room was always littered with ten to fifteen pairs of pants and jackets in dusty, moldy heaps. He told us that he had a $200 monthly clothing allowance that he had to spend every month or it would be discontinued. For him, it was better to buy a new suit than to dry clean an old one. This was my first experience with the upper middle class.

We were all the same age, but, clearly, we were not all social equals. My college classmates' fathers were, for the most part, either lawyers or automobile-company executives. The bulk of them had grown up in the affluent suburbs of Detroit. They believed "clothes make the man" and had the wherewithal to purchase them on an as-needed basis. Both of these privileges were denied me at that time, and I stood apart visibly as a country hick. That initial experience with apparel in Ann Arbor suggested that the class system was alive and well, and I was moderately affected at that time by a sense of not quite belonging.

Some months into my freshman year, I discovered a second important piece of data. I began to notice a small group of people who frequented the Michigan Union. The men all wore jeans, flannel shirts, and boots, as I did, and the women wore long granny dresses, boots, and a large number of beads. Most of them carried green book bags. The men had beards and hair that had not seen a barber for years, in effect making them look very much as if they belonged to the House of David. Despite their hirsute visage, however, I didn't think this was the correct explanation. I eventually learned that they were called beatniks (the direct lineal ancestors of the hippies of the 1960s), and, in outward appearance at least, I fit in with them perfectly. Yet I hadn't the slightest clue what the beatniks were hoping to accomplish. Only later did I realize that my own normal, everyday garments had been adopted by a fringe group as one way of protesting against society at large.

No professor of mine wore Levis to class in 1958, and few faculty members ever did so until well into the 70s. Suits, often tweed, were standard, and it was usually a simple matter to distinguish the faculty from the students. In the fall of 1962, when I returned to college following a long hiatus, I happened to run into an old friend of mine from high school, Denny Baab, who was taking an introductory philosophy course. Denny said that I would enjoy a rather strange character who was lecturing; so on a lark, I accompanied him to Angell Hall. Class was held in a large lecture room, and I was pleasantly surprised when out of the crowd emerged a man with bright red hair and beard who took his place behind the lectern. He was wearing a sweat shirt, sneakers, and Levis.

His name was Richard "Red" Watson. Here, at last, was positive feedback for my own personal dress code. And I have continued to dress in my own way, even for teaching my classes, since that day. Red, now Professor of Philosophy at Washington University in St. Louis, also had an advanced degree in geology. His wife Patty Jo is a superb and well-respected archeologist. Both of them became close personal friends of mine, and later I undertook geological fieldwork with Red in southeastern Turkey during the fall and early winter of 1968. I never told Red what a sartorial role model he was for me.

I am never sure what is in style and what is not since fashion modes seem to change on a monthly, if not a weekly, basis. At least this is the message I get from my own children and from the students in my classes. I often have the distinct feeling that I am going dizzily in and out of style at least twice every semester. And I never know which it is. The word "fashion," itself, derives from the Latin word *factio*, from which we also get the term "faction."

Our clothes transmit to others many things about us, including what group we either belong to or are actively seeking identification with, such as my beatnik compatriots in Ann Arbor. Dress is a form of communication—a way of signaling information about ourselves and our attitudes and beliefs about how the world is, or should be, constructed. With our clothing, we have at least one opportunity to transmit actively, rather than passively, a positive statement to the world around us about our deepest social and personal feelings.

In 1956, Levis defined me perfectly, and probably still do adequately enough today. (Levis, in actuality, did not become popular among teenagers outside of the farm community until well into the 1960s.) In a system of contrasts, they were relatively cheap, uniform in style (unlike the many variations we presently see), mass manufactured in factories, and bought in a common department store. Made of coarse material, they were worn for working or playing. These features all contrasted with costlier and more classy materials for dress suits that are expensive, much more individual in style, sometimes handmade to order, and often purchased in a tailor's shop that specializes solely in men's clothing. Thus, when I appeared in Ann Arbor clad in a country kid's jeans, I was not only out of place. I was also loudly communicating my social status and lower class background to all of my new freshman peers. Yet even today, having learned something about the rules of proper attire, I continue to dress after the same fashion.

I had been duly informed in one of my high-school social studies courses that the United States was largely a classless society. (Gore Vidal once remarked in an essay that "In a sense, midwesterners were the least class-conscious of Americans during the first half of the twentieth century.") And the student population of the University of Michigan is seen by the way they act and dress as still more properly part of the East. Nonetheless, there were some groups of people we didn't normally associate with on a daily basis in my hometown or throughout the county as a whole. These were the Seventh-day Adventists or the Israelites. We typically looked down on them as being of lower status. Yet they dressed in very much the same manner as we did. We had to recognize them in different ways such as their religious beliefs, grooming patterns, or food taboos.

Protest, as such, is and has been for two centuries or more both an important American behavioral trait and an intensely maintained cultural value. Americans have gone through a number of protest styles of dress in their history. These have been classified by scholars as Puritan, Pioneer, and Plutocrat. The Puritans were originally rather a wealthy, middle class of well-educated emigrants who were, in addition, high-fashion hedonists. They dressed accordingly, following the high styles of Europe.

However, with the founding of the Union, the United States began turning its back on many aspects of traditional European culture. Following the Revolutionary War, new cultural forms began to be derived directly from the wilderness (definitely symbolizing the wild or non-civilized, non-European lifestyle). Davy Crockett became the symbol of the properly dressed man, and guys adopted the wearing of buckskin pants and shirts and coonskin hats. (It was surely in accordance with this popularity that the second steamer on the frontier St. Joseph River was named the *Davy Crockett*.)

Then, with the rapid development of industrial capitalism and the final disappearance of the western frontier in the late nineteenth century, finer fashions returned. Again, these styles emanated initially from among the upper and middle classes. Early nineteenth-century egalitarianism, as the American social ideal—which was what I actually had been taught in high school—gave way to multiple status gradings and socio-economic class distinctions. This new ranking system was communicated publicly by an individual's outer garments. Thus, my high-school instruction appears to have been at least half a century or more out of date.

More recently, another trend has appeared. Protest attire has reverted back to another traditional frontier in the personage of the Middle Western farmer. Jeans have become a social standard. Based upon the original and typical farmwork trousers, they now come in multiple varieties from wide bells to flares to straight legs and even in different colors and splattered with bleach or tattered with ready-made holes in the knees, saving the wearer from having to work them in. And small children now wear baseball caps with adorning logos to school, never knowing that this has been an important and functional item of the typical Middle Western agrarian daily dress for up to three generations.

In my own case in Berrien Springs, since the economic level of most families was roughly the same, we all spent similar amounts of money on clothes. The "geeks" or "nerds" (which are terms that we did not know then) and the "jocks" all dressed alike. Levis were the epitome of our wardrobe. In my life today, Levis serve two very different kinds of ironies. First, they were invented, or at least initially manufactured, by Levi Strauss. He has the same name as a French anthropologist, Claude Levi-Strauss, whose work I both admire and follow closely. Second, the original Levi Strauss was born in 1829, the same year that John Pike homesteaded at Wolf Prairie.

On the Field of Battle

*I*n the late winter of 1956, our basketball team was defeated in the Class C state championship game in East Lansing by Crystal Falls, a small town in the Upper Peninsula. Despite the fact that no team from Berrien Springs had ever advanced that far in the tournament (and still has not), it was not well-earned pride in achievement but overwhelming disappointment that fired everyone's emotions for many weeks afterwards. The previously undefeated had failed in the final and most important contest of their lives. Recrimination and finger-pointing accompanied that early post-tournament interval. The malaise lasted well into spring.

Sports provide a prominent theme in American life. They purport to teach us fair play, discipline, and the value of teamwork, hence building our individual characters. Thus, they are more than mere games: They are essential for the maturation of the young. In essence, they are a blueprint for any kid's life, and were particularly so in the 1950s. Also, they are a source of community pride. Hosts of people who might normally ignore or look down upon each other in the streets are forged into one cheering, raucous, unified, and focused crowd. In short, sports are more than simple games that small children and grown-ups alike play.

Our school did not participate in the wide variety of sporting events that are available today. We had no soccer, lacrosse, or rugby. Nonetheless, the most significant sports in our town during my younger days—baseball, football, and basketball—exhibited contrasting metaphors. Each could stand alone with its major value set. Each teaches now and instructed us then. And taken together, perhaps as no other single activity in a boy's daily life, these three are consummately and totally American, particularly the grand old game of baseball. It is not by coincidence alone that baseball is as American as, well, apple pie.

Summer was always the best time of the seasonal cycle. Not only was there no school to contend with, but we could play baseball nearly all day long. One of the most readable books about the sport is Roger Kahn's *The Boys of Summer*, juxtaposing as inseparable boys/play baseball/summer standing clearly in opposition to men/work at one's job/winter. Baseball has been played loyally in Berrien County since 1866 with the formation of the Spear Base Ball Club of Niles. Other early clubs include the St. Joseph Mutuals and their detested rivals, the Benton Harbor Wolverines. In those days, the players lacked gloves and pitched underhand, and catchers didn't wear protective equipment.

My pals and I, as well as countless other youngsters as I later learned, evolved our own local rules. Thus, we could hold a game with only six or eight players rather than the requisite eighteen. In our version of "infield," a ball had to be hit out of the infield on the fly or it was an automatic out, necessitating that, for defensive purposes, only a pitcher and a couple of outfielders sufficed. At the same time, we unwittingly reinforced baseball's important rural image. All of the significant game action was out there, in the outfield—away from where the crowd should be at the edge of the infield to the stands.

Nothing in our naïveté disturbed this rural image that had been constructed layer by layer from myths, many of which even in 1956 were already more than one hundred years old. Baseball's heroes were rural boys: Rapid Robert Feller from somewhere (Van Meter) in Iowa (a rural state) who could throw a baseball straight through a closed barn (a rural building) door; Ty Cobb, the Georgia (which must be entirely rural) Peach (a farm product); Mickey Mantle from another wholly rural state, Oklahoma; and all the players nicknamed Rube, a rural aspersion used to designate country hicks. That year *Time Magazine* described Robin Roberts of the Philadelphia Phillies as a "29-year-old fugitive from the chores on an Illinois farm."

To us, rural as opposed to urban (as in Midwest as opposed to East) was, of course, an essential feature of the metaphor of baseball as America. The game was originally designed well more than a century ago to be played in a park or on an open field; and many of the oldest ballparks carried just such a name: Wrigley Field, Crosley Field, Comiskey Park, and Fenway Park. The Cubs, but not the White Sox or Michigan's only professional baseball team—the Tigers, was the team that I cheered for. On rare occasions, we would go to Wrigley Field, only ninety miles away but about five hours by car in the days before the Interstate highway system, to see a day game. If any ball park typifies America's love for baseball, it is Wrigley Field with its natural grass and ivy-covered walls. Set in a residential neighborhood rather than an urban ghetto, as is Comiskey Park, it firmly links all of us inexorably with the Midwest.

By 1956 we could see the Cubs' games televised in black-and-white on WGN. The announcer was Jack Brickhouse, and the two main sponsors were Hamm's Beer (from the Land of Sky Blue Waters) and HA (Hey Stranger, better get some Hair Arranger). Brickhouse's love for baseball and the Cubs was truly infectious and, since they have not won a pennant since 1945, apparently quite lethal.

Had we been told, in 1956, what I was not to learn for over thirty years—that the first couple of generations of professional baseball players were predominately urban in origin—I doubt that it would have made any impact on us at all. To find out that the fathers of early ball players were not farmers or frontiersmen wearing coonskin caps, but reasonably well-educated, middle-class professionals, would not have kept us out of the outfield on a hot summer day. Even today, when I know for a fact that Abner Doubleday was a graduate of West Point and that he spent the summer there when he was supposedly in Cooperstown, New York (again a totally rural, small-town location) laying out the first baseball diamond, my image of the game remains the same as when I was sixteen.

Baseball, as metaphor, projects America to the world like little else. Much of it, of course, is patently false. For example, baseball was not a path for upward social mobility since most players' families were already up there socially and economically. The myths also hid many facts of American life in the 1950s. No African American played on any major league team until 1947, and even in 1956 integration was token at best. The Boston Red Sox, my other favorite team along with the Cubs, did not have a black player until 1959.

Football is, and was then, totally different. Until 1955, our football team, with its even then antiquated single-wing offense, once held the state's longest undefeated streak. It entered the 1956 season with a new winning streak of five games which it increased to twelve before losing the last game of the year to Buchanan 7-0.

Nonetheless, even once it is over, any winning streak (or a losing one for that matter) can still begin anew with the very next outing.

Rugged, massive, team-oriented football presents quite a contrast to gentle baseball. One envisions coal mines and steel workers (the Pittsburg Steelers) fighting over one hundred yards of muddy ground in a driving blizzard at War Memorial Stadium rather than small tanned boys shagging flies in the park on a hot summer afternoon. Even baseball's typical rituals—booing the umpire, eating a hot dog, or the seventh inning stretch—are peaceful endeavors. The sight of a manager arguing with the home-plate umpire over a called third strike is an expected part of every game's ceremonial performances. It never evokes within us the images of provoked violence that we associate with each play in a football contest.

There has only been one Ty Cobb, a superb baseball athlete whose skills were coated with a meanness that is common among football players. We had more than one violent player on our 1956 football team, such as the guy who believed that he had not had a "good" game, regardless of the final score, unless he had severely injured at least one opponent. But these were my friends, and I consoled them after every "bad night." Such was one of the lessons of two contrasting high-school sports.

But these sports differ, too, in baseball's symbolization of the individual, a true American value. Everything a baseball player does in a game, both offensively and defensively, is subject to a statistic: runs, hits, errors, assists, sacrifices, runs batted in, doubles, triples, home runs, walks, stolen bases, earned run average, saves, and on and on. The recording of assists is a "johnny come lately" in basketball. In football, no such statistic exists. Grunski, the offensive right guard, had 47 opportunities to block the defensive left tackle and was successful 31 times, resulting in 31 positive yardage gains through the run. In contrast to football, America's ultimate team game, baseball—like the United States itself—glorifies every child-adult and offers each one a place in the final record book.

We played both baseball and football at Sylvester Field, a two-block walk from the high school. Left field was the west end of the football field, so a shortstop playing deep in the hole was actually standing in the end zone. We had no infield grass, and neither did any of the schools we competed against. To this day, I am still not completely sure who Sylvester was. I do know that he was the principal founder and president of the Berrien Springs State Bank in 1891 and that he donated an athletic field to the school and the town. One of my old town plat maps records a William Sylvester owning a considerable plot of land to the north of town. Though he was never remembered at any event or commemorated in any way, his gift to the village youth looms up as being far more important than any other that could have affected me.

In my small town, the school year was closely tied to the agricultural cycle. We finished classes before Memorial Day in time to complete the spring planting and well before the summer fruit crops were ripe. Strawberries were the first to be picked, followed by cherries, peaches, grapes, and finally apples. School had begun before the latter two crops were entirely gathered, and the sole high-school sport in the autumn season was football. But baseball, at the professional level, lingered well into October.

In October of the 1956 World Series, Don Larsen pitched his perfect no-hitter. We were not permitted to see this historic game on television because we were in school. In those days, no night World Series games were played. However, the superintendent, Lee Auble, did send out periodic updates on the P.A. system, and the next evening's *South Bend Tribune* featured the photograph of Yogi Berra jumping into Larsen's arms after Larsen had struck out Dale Mitchell for the final out. Even our own then-undefeated football team was pushed aside while we savored baseball's unique triumph.

It is difficult to find a more collective and symbolic memory of 1956 sports than Larsen's achievement. It even overshadows Mickey Mantle's winning the triple crown that year. Other odd bits and pieces come back: Bill Russell and his second straight NCAA championship, the Olympic gold medal, and then his beginning a spectacular career with the Boston Celtics; or the New York Giants 43-7 win over the (my) Chicago Bears in the NFL title game. Yet, the memories of baseball are too sweet. The dreams of equaling, but never surpassing (except in extra innings in the seventh game of the World Series), Larsen's splendid moment still return to me over 35 years later. The closest I ever came to that moment of glory found me crashing into the right field fence (the one around the tennis court at Sylvester Field) to haul in a long fly ball in a game of Infield.

Baseball was once the only sport, and thus it produced all of the heroes for small boys. When Big Ed Walsh won 40 games in 1908, football and basketball did not compete as intensely for the attention of young men, so they could concentrate and perfect their diamond skills. Today, competing dreams of Super Bowl vs. World Series drain a boy's energy before he even knows whether or not he has the talent to engage in either sport beyond high school or even the neighborhood playground.

Baseball, when it was king, also drew father and son together like no other leisure activity. Playing catch in the backyard was quality time, an hour of bonding that could never be matched. Fathers could live their dreams in their sons and envision them pitching a perfect game in the World Series; with their fathers' encouragement, boys saw themselves in a Big League uniform. The future was theirs for the taking. Unfortunately for me, my father left us when I was seven years old and Clark Equipment Company abandoned their factory in Berrien Springs for Jackson, so I never experienced that thrilling emotion.

Sports are particularly good to promote thinking in America. Consider, for example, the nicknames of the teams in all of the major sports from professional level to T-ball. What one characteristic holds them all together, binds them into one inseparable unit? It is not ferocity. If you fear a Tiger or a Bear, try being afraid of a Cardinal or a Blue Jay. It is not occupation—you can be a Meat Packer or a Pirate, but try earning a salary as a Bill (whatever that is) or a White Sock. Even today with all of the proliferation of teams in professional sports—in 1956 there were but 16 major league clubs in baseball—one characteristic still endures, as it has for well more than a century.

Not one nickname is, or ever has been, an edible item. There are no Chicago Chocolate Eclairs, Minnesota Mince Pies, or San Francisco Standing Rib Roasts. There are, and have been, occupations, birds, trees, animals, articles of clothing (Reds from the original Cincinnati Red Stockings) and diminutives (Phillies). We do not eat Rams (but mutton) or Bulls (but beef). Even Buffalo, despite its logo of a bison, is nicknamed the Bills. (A student once told me that a town in northern Illinois had a high-school logo of the Pretzels which made it the regional laughingstock; and I have argued that we do not eat Marlin, although I have been disputed.) Ours was the Shamrocks. Sports' teams are an extension of ourselves and ultimately of our community, and we cannot eat them. We are not cannibals. This structural rule is an inviolable one in all of American culture.

These nicknames serve yet another function in our collective lives. Many of them are wild objects, something arising out of nature. Like the urban zoo, through the metaphor of logos, we bring the wild boldly and directly into our communities. We tame nature through the medium of culture in the guise of our sports teams. Thus, these nicknames allow us to insert the wild directly into our personal lives. Like the pastoral parks where baseball games are conducted, the wild is contrasted with the culturally domesticated existences that we experience daily. Small children can use the natural, outdoor world to dream and to construct their futures.

If these particular oddities seem trivial, and I assure you that as an integral segment of our cultural structure they are not, try the following as evidence for this theme of America. Nothing in sports is ever truly ended. In the same manner as Berrien Springs' Decoration Day celebration, time is conceived of as cyclical and not linear in American sports. The next season is always a new beginning where last year's tail-ender and last season's champion start the new campaign afresh. All are even with no wins and no losses. The past year's World Series winner receives no automatic bid into the tournament to come but has to earn a place in the status hierarchy. You can readily forget last season's dismal and embarrassing finish. History truly does not matter.

Some international sports differ in these fundamental particulars. The major championships, such as the Olympics and the World Cup, are held only once every four years. The World's Fastest Human gains this appellation by winning the one-hundred-meter dash in the Olympics and keeps the title for four years until the next Olympic Games are contested. Olympic champions can bask in the limelight of glory, wearing their laurel leaves of victory for more than three years. And in World Cup soccer, the championship team even receives an automatic invitation to defend its title, having already qualified by winning somewhere in the far, far distant past. Here, history is not only consciously remembered but is taken seriously.

Except for the Olympics, and then even few events in them, international sports had very little significance for my friends and me in 1956. Gymnastics? Crew? Fencing? I had absolutely no interest in the Olympics until I was in college and had the good fortune of interviewing a future Olympic sprinter for *The Michigan Daily*—Tom Robinson from the Bahamas. For us, baseball was world enough.

Even the achievement of Roger Bannister cracking the presumed unattainable four-minute mile in 1954 was immediately undermined when we viewed the film footage of him collapsing in exhaustion upon breaking the tape at the finish line. Here are the contrasts. Don Larsen not only pitched a perfect game, but he also had to carry Yogi around the diamond after the game. Mickey Mantle, bad knees and all, never had to be helped off the field after hitting a prodigious home run. These were our models—cultural icons held up for us to emulate. These men led exemplary lives: no drinking, no smoking, no swearing, no illicit sex (at least, not that we were aware of). Thus, for me, there were no international stars, only baseball heroes.

I carry these memories of baseball strongly within me even today. I lean upon them and use them and reuse them. They are stuck fast as some of the most important events of my early life. Then, we had the Cubs game during the day, and perhaps the White Sox at night. Now, the Braves, Yankees, Mets, and Red Sox—plus ESPN—all compete simultaneously for the attention of my television eyes. I have difficulty not only concentrating but also remembering the last game. In his book *From the Land and Back* about growing up in the farm country of central Michigan, Curtis K. Stadtfeld commented that "boys who have played baseball or basketball through all their childhood have a store of knowledge they do not even know they possess." I recall and I treasure.

Words Move

Not long ago I was skimming through a journal article that dealt with American books, movies, music, and what the author designated as the most significant cult figures of the 1950s. Most of the names were quite familiar, like those of old friends I had not thought of in a long while: Elvis Presley, James Dean, Marlon Brando, Jack Kerouac, Hugh Hefner, Allen Ginsberg, and Mickey Spillane. I heard them sing their songs on the radio, saw them perform on the big screen or, more infrequently, on television, or read something by each of them while still a high-school student. Not one of them could be found in any part of our curriculum. Yet, I have no doubt today that many of them impressed and/or influenced me as mini-heroes, at least to some small degree.

Perhaps, either unconsciously or, much more likely, quite consciously, I frequently patterned some of my own youthful behavioral patterns on one or more of these heroes. Kerouac's *On The Road* was a special favorite, and I read this novel thoroughly several times to the point that it was completely absorbed in my mind. Before the close of the decade, I had undertaken several roaring cross-country automobile trips, emulating—in part—what I thought was one of his essential messages for our most modern of times. One could be a great author and a writer of eternal truths, which I fervently aspired to be, and, in the same instance, could still be completely independent and free to come and go as one generally pleased—unfettered by burdensome responsibilities except to one's art form.

Rebel Without A Cause and *Blackboard Jungle* (featuring Bill Halley's hit rock-and-roll single "Rock Around the Clock" on the soundtrack) also informed us, quite dramatically in fact, that there were other, wholly acceptable (to us, if not to our teachers and parents) ways to behave in public as up-to-date, totally cool teenagers. However, after brazenly addressing Miss Rosemary Good, our English teacher and school librarian, as "Teach" rather than more politely as Miss Good, I learned another hard-earned lesson about bad manners and was quickly disabused of this dangerous notion. Also, I cannot recall that any of my female classmates had personalities that in any way resembled Natalie Wood's in her role in *Rebel Without a Cause*.

A major point of the journal's critical piece was that every one of these individuals had functioned in some manner as a cultural icon. In essence, the article's author proposed that each one of them in his or her own way symbolized a state of alienation. When their contributions were embedded within the cultural context of other more scholarly literature and arts of the 1950s, alienation appears to be a major theme that social critics have selected to characterize the immediate post-World War II era of American history. Reading the novel *The Man in the Gray Flannel Suit* today (I only saw the movie then) and any number of contemporary 1950s academic treatises—such as *The Power Elite* and *The Organization Man*, which I did not examine or had not even heard of until I arrived in college—gives one the impression that almost every American in that decade was alienated from everybody else and everything.

This concept may be accurate for some, but not for all, adults of that time in our history. However, alienation was never overtly exhibited as an overall feeling of malaise or disquietude and neither was it a topic of concern around my household. If my mother, my great grandmother, or even my stepfather Bob—who was, by 1956, steadily working his way up the administrative ladder at Whirlpool Corporation—felt alienated from the world at large, they never seemed to talk about it in my presence. By the mid-1950s, my nuclear family was busy participating in the great American Dream of bettering themselves financially and materially, and they certainly were succeeding. If they were dissatisfied with their present lot or their individual possible futures, they also adhered closely to another typically Middle Western behavioral trait—one of suffering alone and in complete silence. Perhaps they were satisfied because they had not read widely or deeply enough of the current disgruntled literature and thus were poorly informed. We apparently were well behind the academic times in our corner of the world.

I cannot remember that my peers ever projected any active psychological posture of individual alienation, whether constant or even intermittent. We complained incessantly, of course, because our elders did not particularly like our music, hair styles, and slang; and they made us do rather too many chores at home. Still, this seemed normal because, as we were being constantly reminded, adults are simply like that: benevolent, but entirely necessary, tyrants.

Further, they never let us have enough spending money for gas, records, movies, and dates. In his book *The Fifties*, David Halberstam writes that in early 1956 a teenager had an average income (and/or allowance) of $10.55 a week. Nobody that I knew had access to this much ready cash. Five dollars in one lump sum was a small fortune to us then, and some of the money either had to be saved or, perhaps, contributed directly to the family's general larder. The old sentiment "a penny saved is a penny earned" was another cultural value that our parents held, even if they were not overly successful in pounding it into our still maturing brains.

Since we hadn't read any of the scholarly sociological literature of the period, I don't believe we felt truly alienated from the world. My friends and I were not alienated; we were just attempting to forge a new identity without necessarily destroying the system. Such became the prime goal during the 1960s revolution. In essence, what we adolescents understood was simply that we were not yet permitted to participate fully in society's most significant and meaningful material benefits. But we never doubted that we would make it there someday because we were all actively chasing the same American dream. We would not be dreaded Communists, but we would be free, independent, and, quite possibly, rather wealthy individuals to boot.

Material items were constantly being dangled enticingly before us, whether in the *Sears Catalogue* (The Wish Book, which we received through the mail biannually), the daily newspaper advertisements, or the brand-new medium of television. Any of us who watched television at all or read anything—such as newspapers or magazines—beyond what was normally required for basic, minimal homework assignments were bombarded with all the material goods we were supposed to possess in order to be comfortably ensconced in the upper end of the social mainstream. (Betty Furness, "star" of many glamorous commercials, was rapidly becoming an ever-present figure.) I recall that I was mightily impressed by flashy cars, but most new cultural necessities were well beyond my modest monetary means; and, in the end, I never did truly develop any overwhelming need for the bulk of them.

Most of my reading beyond schoolwork, however, was highly eclectic rather than scholarly in orientation. I seldom focused on any one topic for long. Much of my reading dealt with athletics, and the first magazine I ever took on subscription was *Sport*. (This was well before *Sports Illustrated*, with its inaugural issue in August, 1954, that became number one in the industry.) I read *Sport* from cover to cover as soon as it arrived each month. In those days, feature articles were largely given over to basketball, football, baseball, and boxing. Seldom was any other major sport even acknowledged, with the exception of an occasional piece on hockey around Stanley Cup time or horse racing just prior to the first Saturday in May. No crew or curling was permitted! And certainly, because of the moral atmosphere, no swim suits! Within *Sport*'s glossy covers could be found stories of individual heroism on the field of battle and in the arena of real life. Statistics, history, and current events were all combined elegantly into one exciting package.

I even seriously considered sport reporting as my ultimate career. For a short period, during my freshman year in Ann Arbor, I did write on interscholastic sports—mostly tennis, track, and field—and on intramural basketball for the *Michigan Daily*. Thus, at the age of 18, I finally saw my name in print several times a week. I was a published author, not yet knowing that a mere cub reporter was frequently looked down upon by the self-acknowledged, true literary types. Yet, I knew for a fact that Ernest Hemingway—whose career had culminated in the receiving of a Nobel Prize—had started out in journalism. Perhaps I was on the right track.

In Berrien Springs, I did not have unlimited access to a large variety of books, one that could match my overactive curiosity. The Sparks Library did not contain extensive holdings. What was housed within its walls seems to have been heavily oriented toward the more popular romance and detective novels of the day. I browsed through its few stacks continuously seeking new and exciting things to read. During one of these rambles, I discovered for the first time that Berrien Springs actually might have had its own unique past. Several decades later that hint began to jell.

I recall once finding what I suppose today was a basic introductory text on geology. It was certainly a very old one, for it reproduced for extended discussion a seemingly bizarre theory of the earth's history. It was one that boldly hypothesized that the west coast of Africa and the east coast of South America had once been solidly joined together as one land mass. I found the thought of restless, constantly moving continents truly novel—one that never had been broached by our science teacher, John Brawders. I outlined both continents on tracing paper, using a world atlas we had around the house quite by chance, and compared them intently, attempting to find the proper points of this proposed juncture. I naively believed that I had been successful.

However, the author of the text, whose name I have long since forgotten, soundly trashed this theory; then he unceremoniously relegated the entire concept to the garbage heap of bad science from the past. This was, of course, long before the theory of plate tectonics had been developed, researched in the field, and subsequently scientifically verified. This elegant concept elucidates the very physical mechanism which adequately accounts for, among other phenomena, the similarities in the geological sequences, the modern plant species, and the fossil records of the coastlines of these two massive continents. This was only one of the curious oddities one could come across entirely unguided, three days a week (and for free), lodged on the shelves of our public library.

Our high-school library was little better in this regard. Miss Good (who drove a much coveted two-tone green 1955 V-8 Chevrolet convertible), was extremely careful about which books were on display and available for our reading (and educational) pleasure. Occasionally, we would find on the shelf a newly purchased novel in the basic teenagers' genre with some really spicy and juicy parts (one story, for example, was not only of a girl's unwanted pregnancy but also how she got that way described in what was then considered graphic detail). Rather too quickly Miss Good would overhear this lurid sex scene discussed in excited whispers by some of my classmates, and the next reader who approached the novel with great expectation would find, instead, a whole page or more completely blackened out and forever unreadable.

To her everlasting credit, Miss Good did make a valiant attempt, though with little success, to introduce us to more profound world literature. We read some of Shakespeare's plays and Homer's *Iliad* in her senior English class. I found both the plays and *Iliad* to be extremely difficult reading and, quite frankly, not worth the massive effort required for even minimal understanding. Since nobody talked or wrote that way in the contemporary society in Berrien Springs, both authors were quite unintelligible to me. The first quiz that she gave us on Shakespeare's *Julius Caesar* had the following opening question: "What was Shakespeare's full name?" That one was easy to answer: "It was Henry Wadsworth Shakespeare." To this day, I still cannot concentrate for more than a few minutes on anything written by the immortal Bard of Avon.

The *Iliad*, however, as heavy-going as it had proved to be, soon resurfaced in my life. Less than six years after graduating from high school, I found myself on the tell near Hisarlik, Turkey—the presumed site of that ancient and fabled city of Troy. I crawled over, through, and around the still open trenches that were left behind from both Heinrich Schliemann and Carl Blegan's extensive excavations. I remembered virtually nothing specific from Homer's masterpiece—only some hazy and shadowy epic images of the heroes engaging in hand-to-hand combat. This failure on my part only served further to heighten my extreme disappointment in the archeological remains themselves. I am not sure what I had specifically anticipated that Troy was going to be like, but obviously my expectations were not limited merely to badly eroding trenches, sodden backdirt piles, partly reconstructed temples, and massive stone walls. Homer had succeeded admirably in creating some vague, though mythic, anticipations in my mind. Nowhere were they manifested that afternoon in the wet earth along the eastern shore of the Dardanelles.

Once I had begun my own teaching career, one of my first primary assigned courses dealt with the archeology of the Near East. Slowly, I returned to the *Iliad*. But, I think my expressed personal goal was to demonstrate to my undergraduate students how much of the saga was either patently false or, indeed far worse, entirely unverifiable from a logical and scientific perspective. Probably during my third full rereading of Homer did I actually began to appreciate the poem's singular majesty. My appreciation, however, required considerable background reading in the local Bronze Age archeology and history, and extensive theoretical preparation on my part. These background studies were intellectual approaches that Miss Good, as accomplished a teacher as I now believe her to have been, was unable to provide for us in high school.

In retrospect, I realize that one could hardly expect a small-town high school in the 1950s, with a student body consisting mainly of farm kids, to have an academic program that covered anything but the minimum of what one considered the essential topics. Try, for example, prodding an average farm boy into reading critically T. S. Eliot's *The Love Song of J. Alfred Prufrock* as part of his homework. The poem would undoubtedly make little sense to him without considerable assistance from the teacher. In fact, the experience probably would be enough to cause him to abandon serious scholarly reading for the rest of his life. I suspect, with absolutely no offense meant, that some of my high-school classmates may have done just that.

Thus, only faint and hardly active encouragement was given to us to branch out and seek new and fascinating literary or scientific worlds. We had no honors track or even any enrichment courses. We wrote the inevitable and ever unavoidable term papers; but the topics, for the most part, could be satisfied with no more information than could be gathered from any handy home encyclopedia. I wrote a paper on Karl Marx for a senior writing course, and the instructor—our principal—found it generally unacceptable because I had actually discovered that Marx might have had some fascinating ideas. I had failed to be properly critical of his detestable, atheistic perspective. During the Cold War in small-town America, during the mid-1950s, a student had to be extremely wary of Marx and the ever encroaching, godless Red Menace.

Whenever we required additional data for these onerous projects, we normally were able to gather them in the library at Emmanuel Missionary College. Their staff was forever gracious, helpful, and courteous, but I always felt uncomfortable and sorely out of place on the campus. As much as anything else, I probably suffered from a deep sense of guilt over my odious behavior toward the campus community. As a result, much to my deepest regrets today, I never exploited their far better resources to anywhere near their full potential.

Nonetheless, I did read incessantly. In the summer, I sat in the swing on our front porch and thumbed through whatever I thought my mother might not find overly objectionable. Rarely, and I thank her profusely for this, did she ever admonish me to quit reading and get busy doing some real physical labor. For that other reading matter, such as Mickey Spillane's novels or a well-hidden and quickly tattered copy of *Playboy*, my friends had a clubhouse that we had built in Dave's backyard. There, in the darkness by candlelight, I could explore the larger world beyond Berrien County, the urban sophistication of Chicago (at least Hugh Hefner's version of it), and the mean and dangerous streets of New York City.

Thus, both Hefner and Spillane were an integral part of my early education, and I find even today that I could not live in either one of these cities. I realized, through their literary efforts, that there was too much materialism in Chicago and constant and rampant murder and mayhem in New York (where, according to what I read, rain was always pouring down in violent thunderstorms). The images these authors created entirely spoiled my consideration of either city as a future hometown. At present, I live in a small town 150 miles north of New York City, but I do not visit New York or any other metropolis.

A best seller in 1956 was *Peyton Place*. Obviously, it was not made available to us in the high-school library. Yet, somehow, we did manage to obtain a copy. This became another secret book for the clubhouse. Couples really did those joyous things with each other—those acts that we adolescent boys were only beginning to fantasize about. Here, at last, was a true picture of real life in the outside world, and in a small-village setting similar to my own hometown. Another hot book that year was Vladimir Nabokov's *Lolita*. We heard about it, but never could obtain a copy. That, and all of the *oeuvre* of Henry Miller, had to await my arrival in Ann Arbor where my serious education through books began.

Two series I heartily devoured: the Chip Hilton books and Nordhoff and Hall's trilogy of historical novels on the H.M.S. *Bounty* mutiny set in the exotic South Seas. The former gave me a "typical" teenage boy's experiences in interscholastic sports and at high school (how to grow up while both winning and losing the big games and his girlfriend), and the latter provided me with apparently true adventures in an alien marine environment under the most harrowing of conditions.

Looking back, I am mildly surprised that I never developed any abiding interest in the anthropology of Oceania, particularly when I later had access to one of the world's intellectual giants in this field of expertise—Professor Marshall D. Sahlins—while at Ann Arbor in college. Sahlins' theoretical, structuralist perspective would later inform some of my own subsequent research in archeology, but his geographical focus has proven to be forever untransferable. Perhaps it was because my own specialization was, by then, in archeology, and our understanding of the prehistory of Oceania was, in the 1960s, still very underdeveloped. Instead, I headed directly for the Middle East.

Today, Berrien Springs has a new, modern library building constructed on the grounds of my now-vanished schoolhouse. Inside a crisp, fresh feeling is in the air, quite unlike the original edifice that always seemed dusty with the faint smell of mildew lingering over everything. One room houses special documentary collections, and study desks are provided for leisurely examination of the county's past. Overall, it is a clean, well-lighted place. It is situated directly across the street from the 1839 Court House where other extensive records, written and pictorial, also relating to the county's history are curated. My school is gone forever, but the former Sparks Library still stands preserving its memories.

Distant Panorama

*D*uring the mid-1650s, the territory of today's southwestern Michigan most probably held few if any human inhabitants—apparently no one on a full-time, permanent basis. The violent encroachments of the League of the Iroquois throughout the Upper Great Lakes had forced the region's once resident Native Americans to seek refuge westward around Lake Michigan along its far shores up to the present Green Bay, Wisconsin. A few human-caused scars on the landscape might have been encountered by any wandering, itinerant traveler. These unnatural disruptions, extremely minor ones at that, were visible remains of the slowly decaying home villages such as Moccasin Bluff that the Native Americans had only recently abandoned. Their ancient cemeteries holding the burials of their most honored and esteemed ancestors were so well disguised from public view that they still have not been discovered.

The French explorer Sieur de La Salle arrived in the area in 1679 and erected the short-lived Fort Miami on the high, steep bluff overlooking Lake Michigan at the outlet of the St. Joseph River. It soon fell into total ruin. The Native Americans whom the French called the Miamis were just then establishing themselves on this hardly disturbed landscape. Even up through the 1820s, the dozen or so Potawatomi settlements spread along the river's banks, the later French Fort St. Joseph, the Reverend McCoy's Baptist Mission near Niles, and Bertrand's and Burnett's fur-trade establishments had each caused only minuscule modifications to this almost pristine wilderness.

The modern landscape of Berrien County is actually a direct outcome of a cultural creation which first began intensively with the Government Land Office surveys for homesteads and the platting of future towns in the late 1820s and early 1830s. Houses, barns, sheds, pastures and cultivated fields, retail stores, and village parks soon followed in the surveyors' wake. Mature forest trees were rapidly felled for the sawmills, and brush and undergrowth were cleared and burned. In Oronoko Township, the fertile soil of Wolf Prairie was turned asunder with steel-tipped, horse-drawn plows; and future crops, which might range from corn and peach trees to lawn grasses and flowers, were carefully sown. Cattle and hogs replaced the native deer and elk in the woods and meadows. The pheasant was introduced, and the wild turkey was traded for the domestic chicken and—for a while—disappeared entirely from the local ecosystem. Bridges and roads were constructed, thus obliterating the existing Indian trails, and earthen and concrete dams were thrown across the St. Joseph River.

It was a freshly sculptured world, one that was both extremely pleasing and harmonious in the opinion of the new American settlers. After their initial goals of this forced, but in their own minds logical and completely civilized, alteration of nature were attained, the memory of that previously, nearly untouched countryside was discarded and immediately forgotten. The seizure of the land was now articulated as progress.

Once, while I was still in high school, I came across a set of old census statistics and some yellowing, brittle photographs of the town. It struck me that in the late 1800s the local population was around 1,000 inhabitants. By the mid-1950s, it still had not grown beyond 1,500 people. I could easily envision a slightly smaller version of my hometown, but never a larger, bustling, urban metropolis.

The photographs of the village from the late nineteenth century showed a scant two blocks of downtown retail establishments. In the mid-twentieth century, those two blocks remained virtually unscathed and unenlarged. Only two things differed markedly: most of the store names had since been changed through sales to new proprietors, and automobiles and pickup trucks had replaced horses and buggies on Ferry Street.

Thinking about these matters evoked in my youthful mind a sense of timelessness for that landscape which I saw every day and knew so intimately. I naively believed that I could stroll through this same timelessness at my leisure. Both the town and the countryside surrounding the village appeared to have evolved so incredibly slowly, if they had undergone any major variation over time at all, that it seemed to me that they must have been nearly immutable for countless centuries. History had never touched here. Rose Hill Cemetery, the farms with their red barns and their well-tended livestock and orchards, and my great grandmother's house, my ancestral home, all must have existed in this place forever.

Yet, no part of this constructed landscape was much older than a century even then. Rose Hill Cemetery came into operation around 1831, predating even the final naming of Berrien Springs in 1835. The cemetery was strategically located high on the river's uppermost terrace, far above the flood plain and well outside the actual limits of the envisioned town. Still, it was close enough to be within easy walking distance (less than one mile) from the village business district. It was then, and has remained to this day, a rural cemetery in the best sense of the term.

The first consciously designed rural cemetery to be so designated in the United States was actually Mount Auburn in Cambridge, Massachusetts. The facility was inaugurated, like Rose Hill, in 1831. Its creators drew their philosophical perspective from the Transcendental Movement—the idea that an individual's abandoned earthly material remains, from this time forth, were to find their final repose outdoors embedded within nature rather than in crypts or dusty cells inside of or deeply buried beneath the churches as had been the previous cultural practice. Death had come to be viewed in the early nineteenth century as an integral part of what was known to be the normal cycle—life, death, and rebirth—just as we all observe that eternal rhythm occurring annually in the natural world around us.

Yet, these new-style cemeteries were not meant to be merely locations with the sole function of sanitizing the towns and cities through the act of hiding their dead—in effect hastily removing them from the sight of their kinfolk and neighbors. The cemeteries were also conceived of as well-planned natural temples where still-living relatives and friends could visit the grave sites and, at the same time, contemplate and commune with the trees, shrubbery, and carefully tended flower beds while enjoying the fresh air and the melodies of song birds. In short, cemeteries were now viewed as formal gardens.

Mount Auburn quickly became symbolized across the United States as a national treasure—an outdoor school for hands-on instruction about the marvels of nature and a pleasant park for family picnics and rambles. From the onset, it drew thousands of eager visitors yearly, including such famous European tourists as Charles Dickens. The dead were now firmly integrated into every living person's daily existence.

The rural cemetery movement, as an intellectual concept, spread within two decades deeply into the Middle West. Chicago's first rural cemetery was designed by William Saunders and began operation in 1859. It, likewise, was named Rose Hill. A few years later in 1863, Saunders, who by then was employed at the United States Department of Agriculture, drew up the plans for the Soldiers' National Cemetery at Gettysburg which would honor the brave men who had fallen there in battle that summer from both sides of that Civil War. Gettysburg's memorial cemetery was formally dedicated by America's most renowned public orator, Edward Everett, who spoke for three hours. (A much shorter speech of 272 words, lasting about three minutes, was given by President Abraham Lincoln—a speech that many American schoolchildren have memorized.)

Coincidence or not, Rose, though sometimes combined with other words, is one of the most popular names for Michigan's cemeteries. Of the twenty-one times that the name Rose appears in this context in the state, five are Rose Hill. In addition to the one in Berrien Springs, others appear in Eaton, Macomb, Leelanau, and St. Clair counties. A Rosehill is in Iron County.

I was surprised to find that there are actually five additional cemeteries in Oronoko Township. Two of them—Feather (Harner) on Hinchman Road and Salem Lutheran on Scottdale Road—are located near Hinchman. Burke and Oak Grove (Storick) are both along the north side of Snow Road in Sections 27 and 28, respectively. A private cemetery—Boyle—is in Section 31 on Hill Road. I must have seen all of them at one time or another, but I never was cognizant of their existence.

Funerals are an integral part of the social fabric of all small country towns where everyone knows many of the most closely guarded and intimate details about their friends' and neighbors' innermost lives. In such a context, anyone's death, while it may not touch one personally, nonetheless touches marginally because everyone quite likely is acquainted with the deceased or with a member of his or her kin group. Further, most of the village inhabitants, regardless of their social status in life—no matter how exalted or lowly—were or eventually would be buried locally in the family's private plot.

Trips to Rose Hill Cemetery in order to pay respect to the dead included not only those journeys following the actual funeral ceremony but also the annual Decoration Day rituals which have always concluded there. Regular visits took place, too, simply for a moment of thanks to those who had nurtured, validated, or befriended the living. My great grandmother Mary, even to her ninetieth year, would suddenly announce, "I want to go out to the cemetery and see my friends." Even though nearly blind by then, she would walk unerringly, supported by her stout cane, along the grave rows that were so familiar to her. Frequently, she would stop by a tombstone in a location she innately recalled. Tapping it several times with her walking stick, she would call out cheerfully, "Cora, I'm still kicking." In this manner, small-town cemeteries were already places of contemplation before the rural-cemetery movement had been conceived by those early nineteenth-century Eastern Brahmins.

Undoubtedly, one can learn much from the planned layout of any cemetery. Rose Hill has been reconstructed and enlarged in a methodically envisioned manner over the nearly ensuing century and a half. Just inside the cemetery entrance, which, in the mid-1950s, was never barred to visitors by a locked gate as it is today during night hours, was the oldest section of the facility. In its far northeastern corner lies the Pitt Brown family. The Hoopingarners' family plot is situated a few paces farther to the south, immediately abutting the narrow crushed-stone roadway. Here are interred my great grandparents, John C. (1858-1929) and Mary (1866-1962). Their heads lay toward the east in the direction of Lake Chapin and the rising sun. To the south of Mary is one of her two sons, John, my maternal grandfather. John, Jr., himself is flanked by his two wives, both of whom have "Ethel M" engraved on their headstones.

Today, the Hoopingarners silently, but vigilantly, guard the route backwards in time to even earlier settlers of the community. Immediately behind them to the east, again toward Lake Chapin, are the Platts from whom the town purchased the Grove. Next to the Platts are the venerable Kephart and Kimmel families. This is, indeed, a location of honor for my maternal ancestors.

The cemetery was never a place for us kids to fear. Ghosts and malevolent spirits were appropriate for Halloween, but one's relatives, including those no longer among the living, did not engender visions of zombies in the night. Thus, our wild, raucous games could spill from the adjoining woods into Rose Hill and across the grave lots, past the proudly waving American and faded Union Army flags, and then down the slope to Lake Chapin without pause for any reflection. The cemetery would also function, very late at night, as a hideaway for the occasional teenage couple who wished to shut out the world for a few hours of intimacy enjoyed within their car. Thus, even if not a conscious part of a person's everyday existence, this sacred place was not encountered by any of us with feelings of awe or dread.

Lovingly tended orchards also covered the rolling countryside. The first fruit trees in Berrien County were probably planted by French trader Louis Chevalier who was forced to leave Fort St. Joseph in 1780. When the initial American homesteaders began migrating into the region, they discovered, as part of the enduring legacy, a healthy producing orchard. Shortly after arriving to construct the Carey Mission, Reverend Isaac McCoy planted between 200 and 300 peach, pear, and apple trees. By 1834, boatloads of ripe fruit were transported downriver from Niles to St. Joseph. In 1839, the county's harvests were shipped on board the schooner *Henry U. King*, captained by Curtis Boughton, across Lake Michigan for sale in Chicago's eager markets. One ship, the *Hippocampus*, overloaded with peaches, sank in Lake Michigan in 1868 with a loss of 26 lives. As early as 1865, Berrien County could already boast the presence of around 300,000 fruit-bearing trees, and soon fortunes were made through the ownership of such famous establishments as the Cincinnati Orchards near Benton Harbor.

New types of trees had by now replaced the precontact species across the county's landscape. Peaches, apples, plums, cherries, and pears had become the focal point of the seasonal harvests rather than the wild-growing hickory nuts, walnuts, beechnuts, and acorns. In the same manner as their owners and caretakers, all of these domesticated fruits were direct descendants of foreign invaders. Members of the rose family (Rosaceae), apples, cherries, pears, and plums were first brought under cultivation well before the beginning of the Christian era in that vast region spanning from southeastern Europe to western Asia, most likely in the vicinity of the Black and Caspian Seas. Homer sang praises to the pear well before 500 B.C. Peaches appear to be native to China and may have been domesticated in the beginning principally for the beauty and sweet aroma of their blossoms and the graceful outlines of their boles and branches against a blue summer sky. Peaches are mentioned also in written documents dating back to the fifth century B.C.

Thus, the orchard was a new kind of forest, one with nearly straight rows of trees and little if any understory. It was a forest carefully cultivated, pruned, and sprayed by its protectors. Yet, like the primeval woodlands reverently venerated by the previous Native American consumers who ritually thanked their gods for their annual generosity, prayers of praise and supplication were offered also by the farmers to their own God. Their prayers begged for protection from the "yellows" and the late frosts in the spring that might kill the buds, for bountiful harvests, and for the continued growth and productivity upon which their daily livelihoods depended.

Every fall in the 1950s, we would load the cider press on a wagon and pull it with a tractor into Calderwood's orchard. Here, using over-sized shovels, we would scoop the fallen apples from the ground and deposit them into the press. Running the press directly from the tractor's engine, we could manufacture gallons and gallons of cider in a few short hours. We would store our own harvest, without any modern preservatives, in large wooden kegs in Calderwood's barn. After the cider had sufficiently hardened, we would feast on the sweet juices throughout the long winter months.

Any wanderings of mine across the countryside, whether on foot or by bicycle or, later, by automobile, were not entirely aimless for they also took me purposely past these same orchards. There was never any thought that they had not been there steadfastly anchored to this rich earth for innumerable centuries. My seasonal routes were based upon a slowly accumulated knowledge of where cherries would be ripe in the summer or apples in the fall. Like the once primeval forest that graced this land, these trees, too, were predictable, producing their fruits at the correct time of the cycle every year.

Lucius Lyons's 1829 plat map of the future Oronoko Township shows no orchards, no cemetery, and no town—simply the enigmatic Lawrence Cavanaugh's cornfield. On the 1873 plat map of the town, only a vacant space (Lot No. 138) lies at 212 South Main, the northeast corner at the intersection of Main and Julius Streets. Three years later, my great grandfather arrived and soon began operating his own hostelry which he obtained in a straight swap for the Hotel Berrien. This large thirteen-room house functioned as a home to countless individuals over the next nearly three quarters of a century, and alternately sustained and confined me like a cocoon for almost a decade.

My bedroom was on the upper story, at the head of the stairway in the southwest corner. This is the wind-and-weather corner. No forced hot-air register connected my room directly with the coal-burning furnace—only an opening in the floor covered with an iron grate was designed to allow warmth to seep slowly upward from the dining room below. It may be a law of physics that hot air always rises, but that principle had not yet been discovered in the mid-1950s. During the winter months, when the wind howled outside my window, I had to burrow deeply into my blankets to keep from freezing. In the summer, when the Middle Western heat and humidity were oppressive, the maple trees blocked all hints of any cooling breeze reaching me through the wide-open windows. Despite these apparently considerable discomforts, I tolerated everything, for this room was my refuge. Here, I could study and plan and dream.

Family meals were normally conducted in the kitchen. The large dining room was reserved for ceremonial occasions. I have become accustomed to spending large numbers of hours in a kitchen and using a dining room only rarely. Modern tract houses with their postage-stamp-sized kitchens and afterthought dining rooms lack the warmth and friendliness of that old house.

Lot No. 138 had no garage until the early 1950s. Then, when one was constructed, it was built free standing, rather than attached, along the eastern side of the lot. Garages crammed onto the house are an abomination of the automobile age. One side of the garage provided an excellent right-field wall, and the roof was the imaginary right-field stands where a high pop fly ball could safely land and be declared a home run. To take advantage of this geography, I turned myself, through long hours of practice, into a left-handed batter. Left and center fields were spacious, running across the backyard all the way to the next-door neighbor's. The Chicago Cubs won an amazing number of games, pennants, and World Series in that small-town, backyard, baseball park.

A wide porch extended across much of the front of the house. Each spring we hung a swing from hooks at one end and brought chairs out from the garage. As neighbors passed by on their daily rounds, they stopped to chat for a moment. One structural feature of this form of neighborliness was that the passersby never approached the porch without being explicitly invited to do so; rather, most conversation took place at some distance between the speakers. This custom, perhaps, epitomizes the personal space individuals from the Middle West require; too much closeness is studiously avoided.

Here, too, is where much of my reading took place in the summer. From early morning until evening the light was excellent; after dark the overhead porch lights sufficed. Until this day, I still read outdoors, even in the cold and snows of winter. Such habits are for a lifetime and are not to be broken capriciously.

Thus, there are stories to be read in the structured landscape around us. Berrien County is a wholly human creation, excepting not even the morainal deposits and the sand beaches of Lake Michigan. The St. Joseph River belongs to the human past as much as do the apple orchards and hay fields of Oronoko Township, for our species had to define them before they could enter into the natural world. For myself, I strive to become part of my own landscape—unobtrusive and invisible.

We Shall Not Cease from Exploration

I begin this last chapter in my old room in my father's house in Willshire, a small farm town of around 250 people situated on the deep, fertile loess plains of extreme west-central Ohio. This room usually functioned as a den, but it did contain a single couch/daybed upon which I slept during my several periodic visits. My father has been dead for over 20 years, and his widow (his last wife and, consequently, my last stepmother) recently passed away. I have come back here to spend a few days for the first time since his funeral in 1978. Many dreary affairs have to be cleared away.

I spent some six weeks of the summer of 1956 here, entirely against my stubborn teenage will. I wasn't really invited to visit, but was just told by my father how it would be. It was not so much that we did not get along. We were not especially close and were never really good friends, but we seldom argued or even raised our voices to each other. He rarely became angry about anyone or anything. He seldom swore, and he didn't drink alcohol. He did, however, fancy himself a gambler (a semi-professional, I guess) and spent much of his time in Las Vegas playing poker beginning in the early- to mid-1940s—usually with only a modicum of success. I believe that he enjoyed or was emotionally moved by very little around him.

One of his few avocations was baseball. We made two trips by automobile to Cincinnati on Sunday afternoons that summer to see doubleheaders—I forget against whom. Crosley Field, like Wrigley Field, was a park splendid in its individuality. It had the form of an uphill slope just before the outfield wall as the functional equivalent of a cindered warning track. Attending those games is one of the very few tender memories I still retain of my father.

As I sit here, I find myself frustrated by a question: What can I accurately know about the past, even about the one I have lived? After all, I am an archeologist by training, and I am charged with thinking clearly about what transpired long ago. I realize that I have recreated all of these specific events somewhere in the deep recesses of my own mind, but I think that my memory sometimes plays cruel tricks on me for it is extremely selective in its operation. Few are the embarrassing moments that I choose to recall—few the moments of boredom or despair. Yet, I well know that I had each of these moments, and perhaps more, as would any teenager. But I have learned during this journey that only loneliness remembers itself.

In a larger sense, then, I have here created, rather than simply brought purposely back to mind, the hometown of my youth and some segments of its own past—but only ones that directly impacted me. Not surprisingly, I have found that most accounts of the past are personal, saying as much about the author as they do about the subject. I cannot separate myself clearly from my place and its institutions. The traditions of the village are mine, too. From that perspective, my narrative throughout this exercise has been a process of creative imagination.

One of the pioneering anthropologists, Bronislaw Malinowski, commented once in his secret, never-to-be-published diary, long after his several years of intensive study of an exotic culture in Melanesia, that the Trobriand Islanders did not exist until he invented them. Could this island village of mine possibly be a similar kind of invention that in no way is recognizable to any of my former high-school classmates? Perhaps, but that must constitute the subject of another book. I do like to continue to believe that such a place once existed entirely outside the synapses of my own brain, but I still cannot be sure. Rereading these pages breeds many doubts—hence the phrases included in my dedication.

One thing has become patently obvious to me. Nostalgia is a most dangerous emotion. Not only does it crudely discolor and misshape memory, but it also selects from the host of possibilities our personal, individual events—ones that can cause us neither acute pain nor everlasting embarrassment. The past is dead, if never completely buried and, hence, conveniently forgotten. That alone leaves it open to manipulation at my capriciousness. Because of this, I can twist it hither and yon just enough so that the results of my efforts cause me no discomfort in the final recounting.

On the one hand, the world of forty years ago seems to have been one of mobile white males spiraling ever upward. For them, and likewise for me, even with the godless Communists surrounding us, the future was limitless; opportunity was everywhere (if, in the end, only in the fold-out pages of *Playboy*). Further, my local world, as I remember it now, was filled with normally kind and understanding adults. No wonder that today nostalgia is a politically incorrect emotion, for this place and time could not have been perceived in precisely the same manner by all of my male peers, much less by the young women I grew up with. This is the stuff of benign local history which makes of the past a happy Eden, but a paradise that can never again be reached no matter how hard we strive to attain that blissful (and perceived) former state. It remains forever just out of grasp, tantalizing and beckoning.

Thus, the picture that I paint of my youth seems to depict a time of generally great serenity. But I know it was also a prelude to the protests and upheavals of the 1960s, some of which I participated in directly such as the civil-rights protests and the Vietnam War teach-ins that swept Ann Arbor. The 1950s—that first decade of the post-World War II era—saw the seeds of all of the upcoming revolutions that my generation precipitated as it attempted to mature. In ensuing decades, these revolutions exploded into a world that would be thoroughly altered, again and again, carrying my peers and me along with them.

When I moved to Ann Arbor from Berrien Springs in 1958, I entered a university environment that was totally new to me, although I did not immediately recognize much of it as such. It was there that I first learned to emphasize the concept of linear time. Rural life and its small towns, like the sport of baseball, focuses on cycles—the seasons, the crops, and the farm animals and their care. In this quintessential American metaphor, each inning is a repeating cycle: six outs before a single inning of the nine is completed. Twenty-seven individual put-outs must occur for a team to lose the game completely, regardless of how much the hands on the clock have progressed inexorably forward. Both Decoration Day and baseball's All Star Game return on schedule in their own good time. But in the new world I encountered at the age of eighteen, events and people no longer leapfrogged easily through time only to reappear again and again in different guises. Uniqueness became the cardinal rule, and I had to try to play this

brand-new, thoroughly confusing game without first compre-
hending either its goals or its rules.

Today, my urban students, in their discussions with me, seem
to conceptualize rural life and its small farm towns as cultural
entities that are somehow related directly to a nearly vanished
past—individual family farmers to them, in one sense, are living
fossils akin to American dinosaurs. Yet, they misunderstand that
the simple act of planting a crop is, itself, a future-oriented activity. Without this initial step in the spring, one has no harvests to
look forward to in the late summer and autumn and no
Thanksgiving to celebrate.

It seems ironic to me now to realize that it was in that university setting that I first became actively aware of the past as an entity worth thinking about. Education supposedly is designed to
prepare all young people for a better future; without it, no matter
how rudimentary, our possible futures are far more limited. My
high-school instruction, as I remember it, almost entirely lacked
this keen intellectual perspective. I feel no rancor about this lack,
though it does leave me somewhat sad. I believe my teachers
were honestly doing their best to instruct us and deeply cared
about what would become of us.

In Ann Arbor, I first came into contact with the cherished past
of many cultures. There I became actively involved with many of
them due to the tremendous diversity: individuals from a number
of countries whom I could meet, observe, and befriend, but whose
cultures I could not yet reflect upon because I still lacked the
proper knowledge and perspective. I gradually acquired these
intellectual tools and took them with me over the next three
decades to Turkey, Israel, France, Belize, and Peru to conduct
fieldwork, recognizing, if not always understanding, the variability in the world around me.

But what did I recognize? How does it bear on my story?
Certainly, the technologies I encountered varied, being less
advanced in the remote villages of the Taurus or Andes
Mountains. And, too, I was often at a loss to comprehend fully the
languages, although usually I could make myself clear enough to
obtain food, shelter, directions, and bargains in the bazaars and
shops. Yet, within the variability was an underlying structure that
I could sense if not quite articulate. Within the sameness of people
living, laughing, and loving were always the cultural differences
in the way they conducted daily life.

My teachers in the Department of Anthropology, at that time,

were heavily concerned with materialism (although not necessarily Marxism), particularly the cultural evolutionary theory.
Leslie White, the towering giant in the field, and two of his most
promising students—Elman Service and Marshall Sahlins—were
all there. Anthropology was a science, they averred, and cultures
could be analyzed and explained by close examination of their
technologies and the interrelationships of their units of produc-
tion. These interrelationships determined a specific social organization for the human unit, and both technology and social structure together, in turn, required that a basic (and predictable) ideology and religion must be followed. Prehistoric archeology (my
field) as a subdiscipline of anthropology found this theoretical
approach highly amenable. After all, archeologists study material
items—from flint chips to whole sites—and their interrelationships. Cultural materialism was the proper approach to understanding what had already taken place.

Over a three- to four-year period, I noticed that Marshall
Sahlins had begun to alter his approach slightly. He was falling
under the influence of the French ethnologist Claude Levi-Strauss
whose "Dephic writings" (Sahlins' words) argued that, since all
cultures have a symbolic structure, the meanings of the often
arcane symbols could be revealed through analysis of their mythic corpus. But myth is only another, and often more fascinating,
way of expressing the collective memories of a cultural past. Its
narratives, composed of metaphors and set in cyclical time,
impart historic importance to any society's values. Traditions
emerging in the Dream Time have no linear meaning for heroes,
and events are reinvented as the ritual occasion demands. Thus,
where a recognizable structure exists there is also the distinct possibility of our gaining intelligibility. Ultimately, all cultures have
the same basic values, though perhaps with varying rank-
orders—in a simple phrase, different flags around which they
must rally.

When I think back seriously about my home town, I recall
most vividly the host of flags in the annual Decoration Day
parade and G.A.R. and American flags festooning the tombstones
at Rose Hill Cemetery. Beginning here, I could, I reasoned, uncov-
er and isolate the underlying cultural structure manifested in the
cuisine, the clothing, the sporting events, the social relationships,
and the humanly constructed landscape. What seemed so natural
to me as a boy—to eat pork, to wear Levis, to play baseball

throughout the summer months, and, unfortunately, to believe myself to be more than equal to some of those around me—took on new meanings and significance as I grew older and more reflective of the world's variability.

All of these individual practices, I came slowly to realize, had their own singular histories. Many of them far predated the town itself, the American settlement of the St. Joseph River Valley, and the entry of the French fur traders and the black-robed, Jesuit priests. The domesticated pig has been consumed (and/or sacrificed) and enjoyed by some groups for many millennia, but abhorred and detested by others for over 3,000 years. In contrast, baseball, in its present form, is comparatively new, taking its largely modern shape only in the late nineteenth century. Within each of these and other, additional, behaviors, the symbols—those same flags—appear and are recombined to provide order for time, faith, and fealty to family, friends, school, and town.

Within this environment wholly created by humans, two values were subtly impressed upon my classmates and me: individual effort (that vaunted and cherished Midwestern pioneer rock) and self-sacrifice for the future (you must first sow before you can hope to reap). Present time would continue to recycle, ever shaped and reconditioned by the past, but always recreated anew. Our lives would not be forced unwillingly into a linear time frame, thus causing us to forget and eventually abandon the sacred rituals that rendered them meaningful. Each of the seasons would have its distinct responsibilities and its own rewards. There would be a new opening day and a new championship final. Baseball would continue to be more than simply a game that young people play for their leisure to while away the hours between planting and harvesting. It would be a metaphor to carry securely with you until the final flag was laid to rest on your own mound of earth at Rose Hill Cemetery.

Bibliography

*I*n order to write a more free-flowing narrative, I chose not to include footnotes and/or citations within the text itself. The items listed in the bibliography include both those works that supplied the factual material as well as those that informed my theoretical perspective.

Adkin, C. E. (1990). *Brother Benjamin: A history of the Israelite House of David*. Berrien Springs, MI: Andrews University Press.

Armstrong, W. J. (1993). Berrien County's great peach boom. *Michigan History, 70* (May/June), 10-17.

Bettarel, R. L., & Smith, H. G. (1973). *The Moccasin Bluff site and the woodland cultures of southwestern Michigan*. Museum of Anthropology, University of Michigan, Anthropological Paper No. 49.

Blois, J. T. (1838). *Gazetteer of the state of Michigan in three parts*. Detroit: Sydney L. Rood.

Braun, F. X. (Trans.) (1951). Karl Neidhard's Reise nach Michigan. *Michigan History, 35,* 32-87.

Brewer, R., Boyce, D., Hodgson, J., Wegner, J., Mills, M., & Cooper, M. (1973). Composition of some oak forests in southwestern Michigan. *Michigan Botanist, 12,* 217-234.

Butler, A. F. (1949). Rediscovering Michigan's prairies. *Michigan History, 23* (September), 220-231.

Carey, J. T. (1976). *Berrien bicentennial*. Stevensville, MI: Tesar Printing Company.

Claspy, E. (1966). *The Potawatomi Indians of southwestern Michigan*. Dowagiac, MI: Author.

Clifton, J. A. (1984). *The Pokagons, 1683-1983: Catholic Potawatomi Indians of the St. Joseph River Valley*. Lanham, MD: University Press of America.

Cook, D. (1983). *Six months among Indians*. Avery Color. (Original work published 1889)

Coolidge, O. W. (1906). *A twentieth century history of Berrien County, Michigan.* Chicago: Lewis.

Cowles, E. B. (1871). *Berrien County directory and history.* Buchanan, MI: Record Steam.

Cremin, W. C. (1992). Researching the void between history and prehistory in southwest Michigan. *Michigan Archaeologist, 38* (1-2), 19-37.

Cunningham, W. (1961). *Land of four flags: An early history of the St. Joseph Valley.* Grand Rapids, MI: Eerdmans.

Cunningham, W. (Ed.). (1967). *Letter book of William Burnett.* St. Joseph, MI: Fort Miami Heritage Society of Michigan.

DeFrancesco, K. (1984, October 3). The Grove—rich in history, memories. *Berrien Springs Journal Era.*

Derby, R. E., & Coleman, J. (1985). The House of David: Baseball's bearded wonders. *Sports Collectors Digest, 12,* 82-104.

Ellis, F. (1880). *History of Berrien and Van Buren counties, Michigan with illustrations and biographical sketches of its prominent men and pioneers.* Philadelphia: D. W. Ensign.

Ferrell, N. (1956, October 20). Historic articles on Berrien Springs. *Berrien Springs Journal Era.*

Fox, G. (1924). Place names of Berrien County. *Michigan History, 8,* 6-35.

Garland, E. (1990). Early post-Hopewell ceremonialism at the Sumnerville mounds site (20CS6): The Brainerd phase in southwestern Michigan. *Michigan Archaeologist, 36* (3-4), 191-210.

Garland, E. (Ed.). (1990). *Late archaic and early woodland adaptations in the lower St. Joseph River Valley, Berrien County, Michigan.* Lansing: Michigan Department of Transportation.

Geertz, C. (1988). *Works and lives: The anthropologist as author.* Stanford: Stanford University Press.

Graves, W. W. (1887). *Atlas of Berrien County, Michigan.* Chicago: Rand, McNally.

House, J. H., & Myers, R. C. (1986). The Berrien County courthouse square: A sesquicentennial history. *Michigan History, 70* (6), 21-27.

Hulse, C. A. (1977). *An archaeological evaluation of Fort St. Joseph: An eighteenth century military post and settlement in Berrien County, Michigan.* Unpublished master's thesis, Michigan State University.

Jager, R. (1992). *Eighty acres: Elegy for a family farm.* New York: Beacon Press.

Kamphoefner, W. D. (1984). The German agricultural frontier: Crucible or cocoon. *Ethnic Forum, 4* (1/2), 21-35.

Kotlowitz, A. (1998). *The other side of the river: A story of two towns, a death, and America's dilemma.* New York: Doubleday.

Kottack, C. (1991). Contemporary American popular culture. In *Anthropology* (appendix, pp. 441-456). New York: Harcourt Brace.

Lake, D. J. (1873). *Atlas of Berrien County, Michigan.* Philadelphia: n. p.

Levi-Strauss, C. (1967). *Structural Anthropology.* New York: Doubleday.

Levi-Strauss, C. (1969). *The raw and the cooked: Introduction to a science of mythology.* New York: Harper & Row.

Lott, C. (1993). Electric avenues. *Michigan History, 77* (6), 50-55.

Malchelosse, G. (1979). Genealogy and colonial history: The St. Joseph River Post (Michigan). *French Canadian and Acadian Genealogical Society, 7* (3/4), 173-209.

Mangold, W. L. (1981). An archaeological survey of the Galien River basin. *Michigan Archaeologist, 27* (1/2), 31-51.

Mathews, L. K. (1962). *The expansion of New England.* New York: Russell & Russell.

Michigan cemetery source book. (1993). Lansing: Library of Michigan.

Myers, R. C. (1989). *Historical sketches of Berrien County* (Vol. 1). Berrien Springs, MI: The 1839 Courthouse Museum.

Pare, G. (1930). The St. Joseph Mission. *Mississippi Valley Historical Review, 17,* 24-54.

Pare, G., & Quaife, M. M. (1926). The St. Joseph baptismal register. *Mississippi Valley Historical Review, 13,* 201-239.

Peyser, J. (1980). New cartographic evidence on two disputed French-Regime fort locations: Niles' Fort St. Joseph (1691-1781) and Illinois Fox Fort (1730). *Indiana Military History Journal, 5,* 6-17.

Peyser, J. (1992). *Letters from New France: The upper country, 1686-1783.* Urbana, IL: University of Illinois Press.

Portrait and biographical record of Berrien and Cass Counties, Michigan (1893). Chicago: Biographical Publishing.

Russell, J. A. (1927). *The Germanic influence in the making of Michigan.* Detroit: University of Detroit.

Sahlins, M. (1976). *Culture and practical reason.* Chicago: University of Chicago Press.

Schwartz, G. (1970). *Sect ideologies and social status.* Chicago: University of Chicago Press.

Shortridge, J. R. (1989). *The Middle West: Its meaning in American culture.* Lawrence, KS: University of Kansas Press.

Smith, T. (1946). *Missionary abominations unmasked.* South Bend, IN: Windle.

Stadtfeld, C. K. (1972). *From the land and back.* New York: Scriebner.

Stuntz, E. (1983). *The incredible wheel of time* (Vol. 1). Plymouth, IN: Author.

Thompson, P. W. (1975). The floristic composition of prairie stands in southern Michigan. In Mohan K. Wali (Ed.), *Prairie: A multiple view* (pp. 317-331). Grand Forks, ND: University of North Dakota Press.

Titus, C. O. (1873). *Atlas of Berrien County.* Philadelphia: Author.

Turner, T. G. (1867). *Gazetteer of the St. Joseph Valley, Michigan and Indiana.* Chicago: Hazlitt & Reed.

Weissert, C. A. (1900). *Southwestern Michigan.* Kalamazoo, MI: Athena Book Shop.

Index

149